DEDICATION

This book is dedicated to all women looking for their ideal property - one without leaks, liens, or hidden fees. If you've toured Timeshares, tried renovating Fixer-Uppers, or been caught up in Houseboat ownership, this one's for you. Once you read the book, you will under everything I just said.

So, guys, don't think I forgot you. This guide is also here for you--to help find what type of property you really are: an investment property draining someone's wallet? A mobile home that rolls from place to place? Or is your Dream Home on the market? Regardless of the answer, growth opportunities exist-- just make sure that growth occurs on a solid foundation.

May these pages bring wisdom, laughter, and perhaps the keys to your dream home. Now let's talk about real estate-- kind of love! Thank you, God, for giving me the drive and strength to finish this project finally!

TABLE OF CONTENTS

1. **Let's Get Real About Real Estate (Of Love That Is)**
   My journey with dealing with certain properties.

2. **Mr. Timeshare**
   Part-time love, full-time confusion.
   Lesson: Great for short-term fun, but don't expect full-time commitment.

3. **Mr. Rental Property**
   All the benefits, none of the commitment.
   Lesson: If marriage is your goal, make sure this arrangement aligns with your plans.

4. **Mr. Rent-to-Own**
   The Type: Halfway to husband, halfway to heartbreak.
   Lesson: He talks long-term but lives month-to-month. Don't mistake potential for a plan—make sure the lease comes with a real commitment.

5. **Mr. Money Pit**
   A drain on your wallet and your sanity.
   Lesson: If love costs you your peace (and all your coins), it's time to move on.

6. **Mr. Fixer-Upper**
   Potential-packed but high-maintenance.
   Lesson: Only invest if he's willing to put in the work, too—otherwise, it's not worth your time.

7. **Mr. Foreclosure**
   Damaged but not irreparable—if he's ready to heal.

Lesson: You can't fix someone who won't take the first step for themselves.

8. **Mr. Short Sale**
   He's rushing to lock it down, even if you're not ready.
   Lesson: Proceed with caution—love is a journey, not a race.

9. **Mr. Bank-Owned Property**
   Mama holds the deed, and you're just a guest.
   Lesson: Unless he's ready to cut the cord, you'll always feel like the third wheel.

10. **Mr. Mobile Home**
    Always on the move, rarely stable.
    Lesson: Flexibility is great, but stability is better.

11. **Mr. Houseboat**
    Adventurous but lacks stability.
    Lesson: Fun for the ride, but do not expect him to dock anytime soon.

12. **Mr. Efficiency Apartment**
    Bare minimum effort—just enough to keep you around.
    Lesson: Do not settle for scraps when you deserve the whole feast.

13. **Are You Prepared for Your Dream Home?**
    How do you recognize and nurture your perfect match when you find it?

14. **For the Men Still on the Market**
    Lessons for guys looking to upgrade their "property value" and find their forever home.

15. **Can Friends and Family Help with the Homebuying Process—or Are They Just Adding Drama?**
    When to lean on others and when to trust your own judgment.

16. **Closing Day**
    Tying it all together: knowing when to commit, when

to walk away, and how to build the relationship of your dreams.

17. **Quotes For My Ladies**

CHAPTER 1

It hit me like a ton of concrete bricks: could understanding real estate really help me understand how men operate in relationships? At that time, I was in pre-production on My HomeBoyz--my third television show focused on renovation, restoration, and real estate--when the realization hit. So, I immersed myself in realtors and property types; slowly but surely, relationships and real estate have much in common; if someone had told me then that studying real estate could unlock men's mysterious codes, I would have bet them one million dollars, they were wrong-- and now here you are reading my words. I would have lost that bet!

My insights could have spared both myself and my girlfriends much heartache. Imagine having every man come with an individual "property type" listing before diving in; imagine saving time and avoiding heartache by knowing exactly who it was you were dating before diving in! That is exactly why I am sharing with you: the secret language of real estate relationships; whether single or married, this guide will help you find exactly which "property type" your potential or existing partners stand for.

Don't worry, fellas--you are welcome to read along, take notes, and use these insights to strengthen your relationships. However, ladies, this one's just for you - let's upgrade your dating game together!

Before finding your dream home, there's bound to be temporary stays at various locations. Just as in dating, finding that perfect spot requires some trial and error. Once again, like dating, finding one's forever home requires trial and error until one feels right for them. Like love, forever homes are unique to each individual - what might feel like forever to one might just be temporary for another. How can you know when a house is for sale? A "For Sale" sign out front may tell all. With people, though, it can be less clear: signs may show a willingness for them to come off the market quickly if only you know where to look! All clues exist if only you know where to look!

The Real Estate of Love: My Dating Stories

Let me be open about my dating life--an unending rollercoaster of hope, heartbreak, and occasional laughter. Had my love life been listed like property listings do in questionable neighborhoods, it may have started off like one such fixer-upper listing.

At one point in time, I was drawn to men with great Instagram-worthy curb appeal who also displayed red flags that I considered subtle or yet ignored because they were cute.

One guy always had some sort of technical difficulty: when calling him after 9 p.m., straight to voicemail with no text replies and nothing from him until the following morning. When his excuses of sleeping or the phone dying came back, "Oh, I was sleeping" or "My phone died." Of course, I wanted to believe him - who am I to accuse someone else of running secret relationships behind my back? But let's be real--this wasn't season one of CSI, so it seems likely I was being too trusting by giving him too much leeway because it seemed nicer and I didn't want to look crazy! Looking back, though, I may have given too much leeway because of liking his view!

On the flipside were those guys who were refreshingly honest - too honest, in fact! They told me right out that they weren't ready for commitment just yet, but might one day. My hopeless romantic side told me "Well, one day isn't today, but maybe I can help them get there." To my dismay, they never booked flights either; these guys made it clear they weren't looking at commitment in their immediate plans.

I remained hopeful and held out hope they would change; eventually, it dawned on me that waiting was like waiting on someone to change, which never happens. It was time for me to find my nearest exit before waiting too long before someone who wasn't interested enough in committed relationships, and I realized it's better for both parties involved that just to find the nearest exit possible before giving up hope is needed.

At first, I believed in giving everyone the benefit of the doubt. If someone came to me, you started with an A rating, and it was your responsibility to keep it. Over time, however, life taught me otherwise: people should start from wherever they are at (B, C, or even D levels) and work their way up from there; trust is something you earn through hard work; this mindset not only saved me heartache but taught me much about myself.

Now, here's where it got interesting (in retrospect): Some men came on so strongly I seriously considered filing for a restraining order against them. One guy called every hour after only speaking once or twice; his goal was to lock me into an intimate relationship as quickly as possible - in my head, I kept asking: "Sir, are you a serial killer? Where are the bodies?" It wasn't romantic at all - more like terrifying.

Women face a constant struggle between seeking out nice guys or bad boys when looking for partners. We prefer someone who combines sweet and kind with just enough edge to keep things interesting; what we don't want, however, is someone with an extensive rap sheet who requires watched visits or courtroom drama - that would just add unnecessary drama!

Dating can be exhausting. Like playing Monopoly, dating can either land on Park Place and bring in big profits, or it ends up in tragedy (emotionally speaking). But it doesn't have to be this way if two adults communicate openly about their intentions for dating each other. Honesty is key; without it, you risk building castles on quicksand.

So, here's my takeaway: learn to read the signs. Seek out those who value themselves like prime real estate rather than rundown motels, and remember in dating that it's often better to walk away from deals that don't suit than to invest in property that won't appreciate. Navigating the real estate of love may seem complicated at first, but knowing exactly what it is that you want makes the process a lot simpler.

Dating Decisions and the Self-Examination Spiral

Just let me tell you this--nothing beats making a series of questionable dating decisions to force oneself to stop and reflect upon their life. These moments often leave people asking, "Am I the problem?" Were my desperate actions or stupid ones the problem, or was it some hopeless optimist who tried making lemonade from lemons life had presented?

My mind was constantly going over the same scenarios as an

embarrassing sitcom. There I was, giving second chances to men who, upon closer examination, should've been met with swift dismissal from my life. And there were no subtle red flags--these were full-on neon warning signs proclaiming, "RUN!" Instead of listening and acting swiftly enough on those warnings, I instead found myself thinking to myself," Well maybe it won't be that bad after all," when in reality, it always was that bad.

Mr. Do Wrong was one such individual. You know who he is: charming smile and laugh, while underneath all that lies a walking tornado. At first, I blamed myself; maybe this kind of chaos was somehow my responsibility, or simply bad luck? But as time went on and similar incidents kept occurring, I started wondering if maybe an invisible sign on my forehead read, "Come ruin my day!"

Mr. Do Wrong would say all the right things, while not following through. After making large promises and then suddenly vanishing for three days without explanation, there would always be an excuse like illness, lost phone or my personal favorite: "I've been really busy."   When he reappeared, there would always be an excuse like life becomes hectic or "I've just been really busy," leaving me nodding, along thinking, "Yeah, life gets hectic," when I should have asked, "Busy doing what, sir? Lies?"

No one guy was exempt; rather, I had a type. In fact, I could've created an entire museum of Do Wrongs to house my collection: emotionally unavailable men with no intention of dating again who expected boyfriend privileges, nevertheless. I almost felt as though I were running a charity for lost causes by giving out free passes to those who looked good, smelled good, and said the right things at just the right moment.

At some point, I realized it was time for an honest dialogue with myself: was I really so desperate for companionship that I accepted anything that came my way, or was I being overly optimistic in believing these walking red flags could turn out to be wonderful underneath their shell? Either way, the outcome was the same-I kept landing men who treated me like side dishes when I was an entire entree.

At some point, though, one must stop blaming "the market" and look inward. Was my love of romance clouding my judgment, or was I giving too much of myself away to people who barely deserved an acknowledgement text back? Unfortunately, both these questions came back with an emphatic yes to me. Realizing my ignorance had both humbled and empowered me; I wasn't desperate, just needing to recalibrate my standards; nor was I stupid-just hopeful; while hope can be a powerful tool, it can't fix people who refuse to change and can only turn lemons into lemonade if the other person provides the sweetness needed for transformation.

Now I laugh about it, but back then it felt like an existential crisis. I had spent so much time blaming myself for being attractive to Mr. Do Wrongs that I forgot I could stop answering their knock. Here's the truth: being attractive to people of the wrong kind isn't your responsibility; whether or not you choose to entertain them is completely up to you - and I made different choices than other women my age.

If Mr. Do Wrong keeps making appearances in your life, here's my advice: stop blaming yourself; raise your standards instead of accepting consolation prizes as compensation; remember: YOU are the prize and NOT consolation prizes!

It's Funny Now, But It Definitely Wasn't Funny Then.

Let me tell you about when I became a professional red flag collector. Not just spotting them; rather, I was literally folding, ironing, and hanging up red flags like decorative tapestries in my dating life. Had they been currency, I'd have been rich! Unfortunately, though, instead of just ignoring or dismissing red flags when they showed up; rather I ignored, excused, or tried to fix them myself - something you shouldn't do either! Spoiler alert: this approach should be avoided at all costs!

As for me, my date with a man who arrived 30 minutes late without any apology and with an unknown stain on his shirt was red-flagged - yet I didn't leave. Instead, I convinced myself it might just be his bad day and convinced myself "maybe he is having one." (That turned out not to be true - that was just who he was). Also red flagged was his constant references to his former flame as "crazy," though at first, I trusted his claims until I saw how closely they related to my own.

Red flags don't always flash in front of our faces. Sometimes they can be subtle - like when someone "jokingly" comments about how you dress or avoids answering simple questions like an interrogation; other times they're more obvious: such as texting someone named "Work" at 2 am (which could show more than co-worker relationship issues).

But let's switch things around for a moment: it is not enough to merely spot red flags; you also must know when and how to raise the white flag and wave goodbye. I used to think raising my white flag too soon meant giving up too soon or giving the person too little of my time, but the reality is: waiting around for someone who walks red flags to turn green is like waiting for a parked car to start driving; it will never happen.

Once, I dated someone who couldn't commit to even dinner plans, let alone a relationship. His refrain from "Let's see how it goes" meant, in reality, "I'm keeping my options open while appreciating your holding my place in line." Did I stay? Yes. Did I regret staying? Also yes. Ultimately, though, when realizing I was auditioning for roles, he never intended to casting me in; I finally raised the white flag and left.

How can you recognize red and white flags and know when it is necessary? Listening to your gut can help. If something feels off, it may well be. If his words and actions don't align, trust his actions more; if his phone is often face down, he could be hiding something; and if all of his earlier relationships were called crazy, well, you could be next on his list!

But here's the key thing: when you see red flags, don't try to cover them up or convince yourself they don't belong there. Saying things like, "Oh, it's not that bad" or "I can work around this" won't do. Remember: you are not Chip and Joanna Gaines-- you aren't here to renovate fixer-uppers like they are; once flags start waving high enough, pack up emotional baggage and raise the white flag!

Raising the white flag doesn't signify failure; rather, it is your choice to choose peace over drama, clarity over confusion, and self-respect over settling for less than what was best for you. Raising it doesn't constitute surrender; rather, it is taking control of an unhealthy situation in order to get what's best for you out of it.

So, the next time a red flag flutters your way, don't collect it; instead, find and call out any indiscretions, raising that white flag if necessary. Life is too short to ignore signs like these or hope that they'll disappear on their own; remember, the ideal relationship does not require caution tape but comes equipped with green lights and mutual respect.

Are You Willing to Look Honestly Into Your Dating Habits?

Ladies, it's time for an honest discussion of our dating habits. Let's be open about our choices, partners, and paths taken (often to nowhere). Have you ever found yourself drawn back into situations in which nothing seems reciprocated for what was given? Have you been left asking, " Why am I constantly attracting the same type of person?" Or "why do I give so much without receiving anything tangible in return?" Well, this isn't simply bad luck--it's time to change that pattern!

Are You on a Road to Nowhere?

Relationships can be like highways with obvious signs leading towards a shared future; others, however, offer scenic detours that teach valuable life lessons along the way. But then there are those relationships that lead nowhere, leaving one emotionally and financially depleted or simply emotionally spent at the end. At times, we become so caught up in the thrill of dating that we overlook warning signals and red flags. But not anymore; now is the time to put on the brakes, assess your dating habits, and pinpoint why certain types are appealing.

In this guide, we are exploring some of the more often met "dating property types," providing a candid breakdown of their potential benefits and drawbacks (warning: some don't even have any). We're taking an in-depth look at the characteristics, red flags and emotional traps each type presents. You'll gain insight into what works and doesn't work - and when to press "eject" and leave.

Why This Matters

Understanding yourself and why you keep being attracted to certain types is of vital importance when it comes to relationships. Are they comfort, fear, or something deeper that keeps drawing you in? Finally, are you settling for less than what is truly available because you fear waiting?

By the time this guide is over, you'll have all of the tools to:
* Recognize destructive patterns in your dating life.
* Understand when an encounter has become destructive rather than playful or casual.
* Set boundaries that protect both heart and wallet
* Prioritize yourself and your goals without guilt or hesitation.

Cons Artists among Us

Let's be clear: some "property types" don't belong on the market. These individuals come into your life offering nothing more than empty promises and sob stories; these people don't seek love; instead, they want free meals, warm beds, and someone to fund their lifestyle.

Let's Get Going

Starting this journey doesn't just involve dating; it's about taking control of yourself. Examining your habits, learning from experience, and creating the future you deserve are all part of what it means to empower yourself.

Grab a notebook, pour yourself a glass of wine (or coffee on those mornings!), and let's dive right in. Together, we will explore your dating habits, navigate relationships effectively, and take steps toward finding that "forever home." As someone else's dream home, you are more than a choice and should treat yourself accordingly. It is time you began acting like this, it is true!

CHAPTER 2

As I look back over my love life, it is clear that I was always an idealist aka a hopeless romantic.

I gave people the benefit of the doubt without fully understanding who was taking up space in my heart; giving away my feelings before truly understanding who they were, before deciding who should get my trust, and giving myself away like Halloween candy. Had I known then what I know now, dating isn't just about romance; it requires a careful strategy just like house hunting.

Imagine this. When people search for homes, they don't simply rush into buying whatever first comes up and say, "I want that!" Instead, they take their time viewing various properties, weighing their pros and cons, and comparing features before making an offer. Most importantly? They have their wish list ready!

How could I miss this major step? Although you might not get everything on your wish list at once (hello, fixer-uppers), there will always be non-negotiables--dealbreakers--that cannot be compromised upon. I didn't make a wish list, and it showed. Looking back now, it seems I unknowingly dated every "property type." Let me introduce my most memorable--and most common--property type, Mr. Timeshare.

At first glance, he seems like an ideal partner: charming, engaging, and full of potential. However, there's one major stumbling block. He's only available part-time due to work or family obligations. Perhaps having children needs his attention as well, or whatever reason may limit his availability. Whatever it may be for them, though, this might make an attractive proposition depending on where you stand in life. You may prefer seeing only certain days and nights during the week or on weekends or two dates every weekend!

Timeshare partners can vary significantly in honesty; if a mature timeshare admits their busyness while appreciating any time you can spend together that would otherwise go wasted, that would be fantastic! You know exactly what it entails before signing up with them.

However, some Timeshares come with "hidden fees." You might find yourself playing detective to figure out why he's unavailable--driving past his home, scanning social media for clues, or playing "who's texting at midnight?" routine (yes, I have done all these things). (Don't judge.)

There's always the rare Timeshare who's refreshingly honest. They may tell you, for instance, "I'm seeing other people, but I like spending time with you." Depending on your maturity level and outlook on life, you might appreciate their candor or even embrace the arrangement. If you don't like to share, you could decide that this property just isn't suitable.

Timeshare relationships can be tricky because they're neither ideal nor permanent; rather, they provide temporary respite from life's hardships and are great places for short stays, yet not necessarily where one wants to set down roots permanently.

Mr. Timeshare: The Vacation Property of Relationships

Mr. Timeshare has many advantages: he's exciting, spontaneous, and often leaves you wanting more. In the first stages, it feels like gold; no pressure to spend every waking moment together, and those fleeting moments seem magical - like mini vacations every time he comes around! However, like an actual timeshare unit eventually, the excitement wears off when logistics become less than ideal.

One of the biggest red flags with Timeshares is maintenance issues. He may promise that they'll see you soon, but "soon" could mean next weekend or month - leaving you to wonder: is this property really available or am I just renting time in someone else's space?

An Inspection Phase to Spot Red Flags- Experienced house hunters know not to fall in love with a property on first impression - rather, it should be thoroughly examined before making an offer on it. Here are a few questions to keep an eye out for before placing an offer:

1. **Is He Genuinely Busy, Or Playing You Along?** There's a difference between having a full schedule and one who plays games about commitment - genuine Timeshares will inform their prospective dates about their availability while dodgy Timeshares may leave them guessing about commitment status.

2. **Are You Open to Part-Time Love?** If you're looking for a serious, full-time relationship, Mr. Timeshare might not be your ideal match; however, he could be ideal if casual dating works best at this point in your life.

3. **Does He Keep His Promises?** Honest Timeshare owners

make every attempt to keep the commitments they have made; when they says they will call or make plans, they are bound by them unless they cancel at the last minute or just "forget!" But be wary of those who do not follow through or conveniently forget plans you have set.

Timeshares Can Go Wrong

Ah, the heartbreak of realizing your Timeshare wasn't what it appeared to be. Perhaps you overinvested and patiently waited for him to free up more time before realizing he is spreading himself too thin. Or worse still, perhaps other guests are also enjoying the property; or you begin feeling as though some amenities he once provided -- like attention, affection, or exclusivity -- no longer form part of its package.

Here comes emotional detective work: I can admit without embarrassment (okay, maybe just slightly), that during my Timeshare days I engaged in some rather unseemly behaviors: driving by his house, peeking at social media tags, tracking his last online date (I know what I'm talking about if you've ever looked up someone's Venmo history!) etc.

Timeshares can be difficult, and knowing when it's time to leave can be even harder. It can be easy to get caught up in "what ifs," like what if Mr. Timeshare magically finds more time for me or waits just a little longer? However, the truth of the matter is this: if it is no longer meeting your needs, it's best for all involved that to move on and find what will become their forever home elsewhere.

Mr. Timeshare Can Teach Us

Mr. Timeshare may seem like an antagonistic figure, but he can teach us valuable lessons that will serve us well throughout our dating lives. These include setting boundaries, appreciating time spent alone, and the power to say no when something doesn't align with your goals. Timeshare shows us the value of knowing exactly what we want; after spending enough time with him, it becomes clear that part-time love cannot fill an individual with full-time emotions.

Mr. Timeshare can be an unexpected blessing--he forces you to reflect on what it is that you truly want in a relationship. So often when we begin dating without any real sense of direction or purpose in mind, letting attraction and chemistry dictate our path, but Mr. Timeshare puts an end to that approach, like an invisible hand from above telling you: Are you sure this is what you're ready for?

Emotional Costs of Timeshare Partnership
Like any investment property, Mr. Timeshare comes with its own set of costs - both emotional and monetary. How you approach it may influence this amount as well; here is a breakdown of potential expenses:
   * **Time:** You could spend days or weeks waiting for his availability only to find that plans don't pan out as expected. Time is one resource you cannot get back; be mindful of how much of yours you invest!
   * **Energy:** Navigating his schedule or understanding his intentions can be mentally exhausting; relationships should provide energy rather than leave us exhausted.
   * **Self-Worth:** Without careful thought and consideration, it can be easy to begin questioning whether you're enough. (Why doesn't he make more time for me? Am I not a priority?) However, here's the truth: his availability has nothing to do with your worth and everything to do with his circumstances.

Timeshares Can Teach Us About Boundaries

One of the greatest gifts a Timeshare offers its members is an opportunity to set up clear boundaries. If you tend to give too much in relationships, dating a Timeshare forces you to reevaluate that habit; asking yourself tough questions such as:

* Am I comfortable with his level of availability?

* Am I giving too much of my time and energy away to this relationship which can help establish some valuable boundaries?

* Am I Honoring My Own Needs in This Relationship?

Boundaries exist to protect what's most precious in relationships, which means YOU. Dating Mr. Timeshare teaches you to set clear boundaries and advocate for yourself to the greatest degree possible.

One of the hardest lessons to learn is managing the tension between hope and reality. With Mr. Timeshare, it can be tempting to get caught up in the hope that things will change; maybe he will become less busy, prioritize me more, or change his approach altogether; perhaps this arrangement can eventually turn into something long-term?

But here's the truth: renovating a Timeshare into your Forever Home if that isn't meant to be is impossible. Hope can be powerful, but not a reliable strategy; Mr.Timeshare teaches us to step back and assess things as they really are--rather than hoping they could become so.

Pros of Dating a Timeshare

Freedom and Independence

If you value having some freedom and independence in life, Mr.

Timeshare could be ideal. He doesn't monopolize all your time, giving you room to pursue your own goals, friends, and passions with confidence.

> **Why it works**: By having both options, you get the best of both worlds--a relationship that doesn't consume all your time while still offering companionship when it fits your schedule.

Low Pressure

One advantage of dating for short periods is reduced pressure or expectations, which makes it easier to enjoy dating without feeling overburdened with long-term implications.

> **Why it Works**: Mr. Timeshare can be an ideal choice if you're not ready for an exclusive relationship or simply looking to enjoy life and have some fun in the moment. His laid-back approach may prove refreshing.

Create Intensely Memorable Moments

What's great? With limited time together, every meeting feels special and memorable. Your partner should make every effort to maximize shared experiences for an exciting and enriching relationship experience.

> **Why it Works:** Time constraints often heighten appreciation, making your interactions feel more meaningful and intentional.

Opportunities for Reflection

It's amazing: Being apart gives us time to think. Without the constant presence of our partner, you have space to consider our needs, desires, and whether this relationship aligns with your goals.

> **Why It Works:** Keep your independence while supporting a balanced perspective through this method.

Suited for Busy Lifestyles

What makes him ideal: If your life is equally demanding--whether that be career, hobby or family obligations--his limited availability could fit right in with yours.

Cons of Dating a Timeshare

1. Unpredictability
2. The challenge: His busy schedule only makes him available at certain times, which makes planning and consistency challenging.

Why it can be challenging: For people who value stability and predictability, Mr. Timeshare may leave them feeling frustrated or unfulfilled.

Emotional Ambiguity

The Problem: Limited time together can make it more difficult to find his true feelings or intentions, such as whether this relationship should remain high on his priority list or be treated like another priority in his life.

Why it can be challenging: Uncertainty can create emotional strain and make one question whether their relationship holds equal significance for him as it does for them.

Feeling Like an Option

The Issue: If your love interest has multiple priorities that require their time (work, hobbies, or romantic partnerships), you could become just another task on his list of things to do.

Why it is difficult: No one wants to feel like an afterthought in a romantic relationship.

The Detective Game

When someone's schedule is unpredictable, it can be easy to become caught in a detective game. Attempts at uncovering what someone is up to can quickly become addictive.

Why is it challenging: Spending emotional energy wondering and spying (e.g., drive-by or social media stalking) on other people's business can wreak havoc on both your self-esteem and peace of mind.

Limited Growth Potential

The Problem: If your relationship only exists as occasional encounters, its depth might remain unchanged over time, and it might feel like your bond stays superficial and casual forever.

Why it's Difficult: If you're seeking something more substantial, his inaccessibility could hinder its progress.

Risk of Misaligning Expectations

The Problem: Your belief may differ from his; perhaps you see the relationship as something meaningful and long-term, while he views it more as a convenient, part-time arrangement.

This makes communicating effectively difficult, as without clear dialogue, you could end up investing more emotionally than they're willing to, leading to heartbreak and unnecessary upsets.

Timeshares Can Bring Joy

Timeshares should be looked upon with gratitude; even though they're not meant to be homes for life, they serve an invaluable purpose - offering moments of pleasure, life lessons, and sometimes leading to stronger relationships in the long run.

Timeshares can provide couples with a comfortable weekend escape - not exactly where you want to live. but just what is necessary at that point in time. When it's time to move on, you will come away with greater clarity about what you want and a stronger resolve to pursue it.

Problem: Your view may be of a relationship as something meaningful and long-term, while he may see it a as more convenient and part-time arrangement.

Why it's hard: Without open communication between both of you, investing more emotionally than they're willing to return could lead to heartache in either direction.

Should You Date a Timeshare?

Who It Suits: Independent women who appreciate having space and aren't seeking long-term commitment; and people with busy lives who are open to dating someone more casual or flexible.

Who Should Consider Dating Carefully:

Women who enjoy high-quality moments without needing constant involvement.

Who Should Proceed with Caution? Those seeking stability, predictability, or a clear path towards long-term commitment.

People who become emotionally attached quickly and require regular communication to feel secure. Anyone uncomfortable with ambiguity or who find themselves competing against other priorities.

Final Thoughts on Mr. Timeshare

Mr. Timeshare reminds us that love is an investment; taking risks may pay off, but walking away when returns don't justify them is also acceptable. No matter whether the experience leaves us laughing, learning, or with regrets behind it. Each encounter with Mr. Timeshare brings us one step closer to finding that property and partner who are right for us all.

So, would I recommend dating a Timeshare? Absolutely. If it fits with your lifestyle and expectations. A vacation romance may just be what's needed to remind yourself that you deserve more in life. Just as with real- timeshares, be sure to read the terms before signing on the dotted line, as well as keeping an eye out for better properties later down the line.

Be honest, ladies: when someone said their grandfather "was a rolling stone," they could just as easily have meant "Papa was a timeshare." You know who I'm talking about--he only seemed available during weekends for short stays (not longer stays!) with just enough activity going on to keep them guessing!

Let's change the subject: can ladies be Timeshares too? Certainly! However, they call us something else when we do it; there's simply no equal treatment when it comes to having fun without commitment.

So, if you choose to be a Timeshare, do it without apology. Remember: double standards exist, but who cares? Timeshares know how to maximize their time; honey, you have better things to worry about than worrying about what others think of you!

Are we ready to get this thing moving again? Where is your "Out of Office" sign? Let's keep moving!

CHAPTER 3

Next comes an often complex but mutually beneficial type of relationship: rental properties without ownership.

They can feel cozy, convenient, and ideal depending on where each partner stands mentally and emotionally which may make living together an attractive option; in particular, not everyone wants marriage; for some, it works out perfectly, while for others, it becomes an incremental path toward one big question that never gets asked!

Every friend group has one: those couples that have been together for years--possibly even decades. They do everything married couples do, sharing a home, splitting bills, attending family gatherings together and raising children as one unit. It seems like a forever kind of love, even though they never actually get married!

Some couples may find a relationship like this ideal; if you aren't into traditional wedding vows and traditions, a Mr. Rental Property might just be what's needed. You get all the companionship, exclusivity, and stability without legalities of ownership weighing you down. But here is where it gets tricky - what happens when one partner starts yearning for more? After paying all that metaphorical rent while investing both physically and emotionally into this property, only to realize you won't receive ownership rights?

Meet Mr. Rental Property: the partner who's perfectly content living in relationship limbo. For some, Mr. Rental Property could be their perfect match; for others, he could be an unfulfilling relationship bomb waiting to go off.

The Appeal of Mr. Rental Property

Let's first understand why Mr. Rental Property might appeal. At first glance, everything about him appears perfect - no rush, pressure, or social expectations pushing into an agenda; simply enjoy each other's company without worrying about paperwork, prenups, and invitation colors for your wedding!

Emotionally independent and nontraditional individuals find him the ultimate catch, providing all the benefits of a partnership without legalities or labels limiting it. And for some time, it has worked magnificently well! However, relationships can be tricky. Rental properties come with their own set of terms, and if you aren't careful enough, it might become apparent too late that while you put in all this hard work to make your house your home, in reality, you don't actually own it--never will!

The Hidden Costs of Renting Love

Renting love may come with hidden costs that you might not initially expect. Over time, subtle red flags might appear:

Emotional Wear and Tear: While you might long for "forever," Mr. Rental Property might only see past "now."

Insufficient Growth: Your commitment is going into building up the relationship, yet they're coasting in the present.

Unspoken Expectations: If marriage is something you want, but it has been made clear it is off the table, resentment could form quickly if it creeps in unknowingly.

When Renting Isn't Enough

Mr. Rental Property may not always be bad; for someone not interested in marriage or legal commitments, renting may be perfect; however, for others who envision marriage and vows as part of their future plans, Mr. Rental Property could become an obstacle that leads to heartache down the line.

Mr. Rental Property Can Teach Us an Important Lesson

Mr. Rental Property will teach us one essential lesson: be aware of your non-negotiables. If marriage is something you want, don't settle for relationships that don't allow it; but if a certain arrangement meets your needs without changing anything further - embrace it wholeheartedly--just with eyes wide open! Relationships, like properties, require compatibility. Not every rental property will suit every person - for some, it might just be their dream home!

First, everything with Mr. Rental Property may feel effortless: building a life together, enjoying each other's company; and keeping things straightforward. But over time, certain signs may arise that make you question whether this investment truly belongs to you - things such as perpetual lease renewal. Here's what to watch out for:

1. **Every time your relationship reaches the next stage, Mr. Rental Property finds an excuse not to buy.**

    * **What it looks like:** He repeatedly makes statements like: "We don't need a piece of paper to show our love" and "Let's keep things as is; it seems to work just fine."

    * **Why it's a red flag:** Although not wanting marriage is perfectly fine, problems arise when one partner holds onto hope that won't materialize. If their words or actions never reflect your long-term goals, it could be time to question

whether both partners truly share similar ideals.

2. Investment Without Ownership

You've invested your heart, energy, and time into this relationship, but feel as if all the hard work falls on your shoulders alone.

* **What It Looks Like:** Despite making sacrifices, sharing responsibility, and offering more financial contributions than before, your relationship still feels one-sided - you benefit from his efforts without offering deeper commitment in return.

* **Why it's a red flag**: Partnership is essential in relationships; otherwise, they risk feeling more like tenant/landlord relationships in which you do all the "work" while they reap all the benefits. If he's not matching your investment, then perhaps it's time for reconsideration.

3. Excuses over Change

Mr. Rental Property usually has an excuse as to why now may not be an ideal time for making major modifications to his property.

* **What It Looks Like**: He may say things such as, "Let's wait until we are more financially stable" or, "Marriage is just another label; why ruin what works for us now?" These excuses can last months, years, or even decades before making their move.

* **Why It Is a Red Flag**: While these excuses may initially seem valid, if they persist, it could be an indicator that he's no longer interested in moving forward.

4. Ambiguity About the Future

Discussing his future either causes him to shirk away from such conversations altogether or simply disappears without explanation.

* **What It Looks Like**: When discussing marriage, children, or any long-term plans with Mr. Rental Property he becomes defensive or tries to change the subject altogether by deflecting. "Why are you worrying about that now? Let's just enjoy life as it unfolds before us" is often heard as an excuse by Mr. Rental Property.

* **Why it's a red flag**: When someone doesn't discuss their ideal future vision for themselves or the relationship, it can be seen as a warning sign. If your ambitions include growth while his don't, this shows a fundamental mismatch that's unsatisfying for both parties involved.

5. The "As-Is" Clause

Rental Property often comes with an implicit agreement: accept him in its present condition without making upgrades.

* **What it Looks Like**: He resists serious discussions about improving their relationship or addressing issues; insisting on everything is fine as-is and resisting change.

* **Why it is a red flag**: While no one should try to "fix" their partner, growth and adaptability are essential ingredients of a healthy relationship. If they refuse to work through challenges or adjust, it could result in disillusionment and stagnation within the partnership.

6. The Forever Tenant Attitude

Seems perfectly content to still be a renter without ever considering more permanent arrangements.

* **What This Looks Like**: After being together for years, nothing changes despite subtle hints or statements regarding your desire for marriage - whether that means dropping subtle hints, having conversations or outright declaring your desire - including conversations between both of you about how satisfied he is in where things currently stand and assumes

you will also remain content in where things currently stand.

* **Why it should be considered a red flag:** If marriage or a deeper commitment is important to you, staying with someone who doesn't share this goal could result in frustration, disappointment, and feeling like time has been wasted.

How to Navigate These Red Flags

  * **Engage in an Honest Dialogue:** State your goals openly and inquire as well, without trying to pressure him, in order to assess if your visions align.

* **Set a Timeframe**: If you want more, set a realistic timeline. How long are you willing to wait before giving up hope?

* **Recognize When It Is Time to Move On:** If he refuses to meet you halfway or consider your needs, it could be time for a property that meets these long-term goals.

Mr. Rental Property isn't inherently wrong; he simply stands for one type of relationship. For someone who does not believe in marriage or prefers less traditional lifestyles, renting can be ideal; for others who dream of marriage vows or long-term commitment, Mr. Rental Property is only a temporary solution to an ultimate longing.

Imagine renting your apartment as the idyllic space you admired during your 20s: charming, well-located, and perfectly suitable. But after some time passes, it no longer serves its intended purpose; eventually, you need somewhere of your own where roots can take root and the future can be built - no matter how cozy it may feel now.

When is It Time to Move On?

If your relationship feels like renting, with little return in terms of emotional growth or equity gain, then it may be time to evaluate your next steps and move on. Ask yourself these three questions:

* Am I staying because it is easier than leaving?

* Am I afraid to start again?

* Am I hoping he'll change, even though it has become clear he won't?

Breaking up is scary, but sometimes leaving is the only way to open up space for something better. Your dreams and goals deserve a partnership in which both partners embrace them with enthusiasm instead of making excuses or offering excuses as justifications. Mr. Rental Property provides us with one of the greatest lessons of love: knowing your worth. Don't be misled into thinking that relationships require sacrifice when in reality they should never require that of either party involved - your relationships should support, not limit, your dreams.

Keep this in mind when searching for your perfect rental property match: finding someone whose goals align with yours are more important. If Mr. Rental Property doesn't fit this mold, don't be intimidated into staying with him just to settle the bill for another tenant! If this person doesn't meet that criterion, then don't be afraid to move on quickly!

Dating Mr. Rental Property doesn't need to be a negative experience; for the right person, his laid-back nature may make for an ideal partner. On the other hand, for those seeking something deeper, he may serve as a reminder not to settle for less than what you truly desire. Before signing that metaphorical lease agreement, ask yourself these two questions: Am I planning to live here long-term, or am I just waiting for a question that won't even come?

Relationships, like homes, should reflect your values, dreams, and the life you wish to build. While renting may seem like an appealing and low-maintenance solution at first, especially for someone not sure what they want from life or property ownership yet-- over time the question must arise if this arrangement truly meets all your needs and expectations? As soon as long-term renting becomes the default setting, you must ask yourself this question: Am I truly content renting instead of owning something tangible and lasting?

Say It Loud and Proud: "I'm a Renter!"

Hey, if you love being a renter, own it, girls, say it loud and proud! There's no shame in enjoying the flexibility and freedom of a relationship with no long-term commitments. But doesn't the cost of rent go up every year? I'm just saying!

And unlike in real rentals, where a landlord would typically take responsibility for anything that goes wrong in terms of plumbing or AC unit repair, in this relationship, you are the landlord--if anything breaks, it falls to you to fix or patch it long enough to keep things running smoothly.

Before renewing that lease for another year, ask yourself whether this tenant is worth my investment, or are they just high-maintenance tenants taking up space in my heart. After all, not every renter still deserves to be rent-free forever.

CHAPTER 4

Ladies, are you tired of dating people who offer no guarantees?

Allow me to introduce Mr. Rent-to-Own: an option-filled relationship type who gives you time and space before taking the plunge forever. Unlike guys who leave you guessing endlessly about marriage possibilities, Mr. Rent-to-Own doesn't take them off the table right away; unlike them, he's open to exploring them as possible long-term commitment, but not too quickly either; thus, giving you ample time to assess things before diving headfirst into forever.

Think about it like this: In a rent-to-own agreement, you begin as a renter paying rent and seeing if the space fits with your life. Over time, part of what you invest goes toward ownership if everything aligns. If it feels right and everything fits, finish the deal and make it official as yours; otherwise, you can walk away without feeling like years have been lost on "what ifs."

Mr. Rent-to-Own gives you the experience of building life together while providing flexibility to decide whether it's time for a long-term commitment or just temporary settling in. A relationship on your terms provides time to grow, explore, and decide whether this property is for the long haul or just temporary stay.

Mr. Rent-to-Own Can Be Enticing

* **Enjoy the Best of Both Worlds:** With Mr. Rent-to-Own, you aren't tied into a long-term commitment at once if both parties feel it's right - yet both can make decisions independently about what's right.

* **Transparency:** Both you and he understand your expectations up front; no one is keeping you waiting, and both parties acknowledge this relationship is leading towards something worthwhile.

* **Time for Reflection and Decision-Making:** Don't feel pressured into making a long-term commitment during the honeymoon phase - give yourselves enough time to experience life together first before making any final determinations.

Women looking for something different than dead-end relationships will find Mr. Rent-to-Own an attractive choice. While serious enough about commitment, he allows you to oversee deciding if he truly is "the one."

Pros and Cons of Rent-to-Own Love

1. **You Retain Control:** Without feeling pressured or rushed to make decisions quickly or decisively. Investing time and energy into assessing whether this relationship could develop into a long-term commitment or otherwise.

2. **Clarity:** While commitment may exist, it should not be seen as blindly taking an uncertain step without considering all possible outcomes.

Con: Not Guaranteed: Although chances may exist that things won't pan out in the end, it doesn't guarantee it won't.

Potential Conflict: Without clear boundaries in place, dating could quickly turn into something much deeper and potentially irretrievable.

3. **Emotional Costs:** Any time someone decides not to move forward with an agreement that was only ever intended as temporary can feel like a betrayal and should be handled carefully to minimize emotional costs.

4. **Set Expectations Early**: As with any contract, expectations need to be set early on. Have an open discussion on where each of you see this relationship heading and what outcomes they you for from it.

5. **Check Your Progress**: Take regular time to check in with both you and your partner to see whether things are moving in the desired direction and whether both parties are making equal contributions.

6. **Know When to Walk Away**: If this property doesn't feel right for you, don't be intimidated into entering into the contract; walking away early could save a great deal of heartbreak in the future.

Are You Wondering If Rent-to-Own Is Right for You?

While Mr. Rent-to-Own may have his appeal, not everyone may find him suitable. As with any property investment venture, rent-to-own relationships bring their own set of unique challenges that might not meet everyone's needs or preferences - here is an idea of the types of women who may have difficulty with this arrangement:

1. The Goal-Oriented Planner

For women with a detailed life plan containing timelines, milestones, and vision boards in place, renting may seem like an extra burden on top of everything else they already have planned out for themselves. Mr. Rent-to-Own could prove an obstruction on that path to happiness.

* **Why it is difficult:** To keep on track towards a marriage or family timeline, having clear goals and tangible measures of progress is important to you. A relationship that doesn't provide such guarantees can leave you feeling stuck or uncertain, leaving an important milestone on its timeline uncertainly fulfilled.

* **What to Consider:** If having a firm commitment by a certain age or stage is important to you, Mr. Rent-to-Own might not meet those needs.

2. The "All in or All Out" Woman

Some women view relationships on an either/or scale: either you are fully committed, or it's time to move on. If this sounds familiar to you, a "trial period" might feel unnecessary and even disingenuous.

* **Why It Is Difficult:** Putting yourself out there could feel like evaluating the waters, showing a lack of trust or faith in a potential relationship's potential. You might find yourself asking, if he doesn't trust me now, will he ever?"

* **Keep this in mind:** If you want someone who's willing to commit fully from the outset, renting-to-own may make you feel undervalued or uncertain of their position in your life.

3. The Emotional Investor

If you tend to invest emotionally in all relationships, Mr. Rent-to-Own could leave you feeling exposed.

* **Why it's challenging:** Rent-to-own requires emotional detachment first, enabling both parties to gauge the relationship without taking an irrevocable leap into full commitment. For someone who firmly loves and invests

wholeheartedly, this dynamic may feel constraining or uncomfortable - like dating withheld from romance novels!

* **What to Consider:** If you know you must put forth 100% effort when entering any relationship, this arrangement may prove emotionally taxing.

4. The Security Seeker

Do you prioritize certainty over risk? If that's the case for you, renting from Mr. Rent-to-Own might seem like too big an adventure for you to undertake.

* **Why it is difficult:** To know where you stand and where your relationship is headed, renting-to-own can feel more like instability than stability, leaving you unnerved by uncertainty over its future course.

* **What to Consider**: If ambiguity leaves you unsettled, perhaps a more straightforward commitment would better meet your needs.

Knowing Yourself Is Key

Mr. Rent-to-Own offers women who are open to exploration and comfortable with flexibility an exciting choice, but no single solution fits everyone. Knowing yourself--your needs, goals, and non-negotiables--is of paramount importance in selecting a proper plan. If you value taking time and assessing all your options carefully, Mr. Rent-to-Own could provide the support that's necessary for fulfilling your life experiences. However, others who require certainty and structure as soon as possible, Mr. Rent-to-Own might not offer enough substance to feel fulfilled in life.

Not every property will suit every buyer, which is perfectly okay; relationships like real estate offer many choices to fit every lifestyle; what matters is finding one that feels like home for you. So, if Rent-to-Own might not be for you, don't get discouraged. Keep looking, learning, and keeping faith that the property of your dreams awaits your name on its deed.

Dating a Rental Property

Dating someone who offers all the advantages and drawbacks of long-term relationships without legal or emotional commitment can be both liberating and frustrating, so let's explore its pros and cons in greater depth.

Pros of Dating Rental Properties

1. Low Commitment, High Adaptability

This relationship offers low commitment with plenty of flexibility if long-term commitment is difficult for you; unlike marriage, renting property provides all the benefits without the legalities and pressure.

2. Room for Growth

You can enjoy companionship and exclusivity, without making too firm of commitments too early on in the relationship.

3. No Pressure, Just Results

When dating without marriage in mind, the emphasis can shift more freely on personal growth while exploring each relationship at its own pace.

If you're not ready to jump headfirst into something permanent, rental property relationships offer the ideal way to test out relationships without feeling pressured to jump into something more permanent right away.

4. Financial Independence

This arrangement usually doesn't involve merging finances or sharing assets among partners - making the whole relationship simpler!

Why it works: Keeping financial independence can be both liberating and relieving stress.

5. No Pressure of "Forever"

For someone who doesn't subscribe to traditional marriage or simply isn't ready, dating Mr. Rental Property removes the social expectations for marriage on a timeline.

Why it works: By enjoying your relationship for what it is without feeling pressured into taking further steps, you can enjoy its full benefits without being forced into taking an added step.

6. Shared Responsibilities Without Title

It can be wonderful when two people can share life without legally being bound together, such as splitting bills, making joint decisions, and raising children together.

Cons of Dating Rental Properties

1. Lack of Long-Term Security

The key drawback of dating a rental property relationship is its lack of long-term security. There are no legal or formal commitments, leaving you feeling exposed about the future.

Why this can be hard: For someone who appreciates security and certainty, this arrangement might feel unstable or temporary.

2. Risk of Emotional Burnout

The danger lies in investing too heavily in your relationship - either emotionally, financially or otherwise - without being sure whether it will lead to long-term commitment.

Why it can be challenging: If marriage is something you secretly desire, an arrangement like this one could eventually lead to resentment and heartache between both of you.

3. Misaligning Expectations

An issue with misaligning expectations between you and him: for instance, one may want marriage while the other does not see this path ahead as attractive - this difference in vision could create tension or unmet expectations that lead to disappointment in both directions.

Why it is Hard: Finding full security in a relationship where the goals do not coincide is often difficult, particularly if one party puts forth effort for something they do not see coming.

4. "Almost, But Not Quite" Feeling

Problem: Even though you might enjoy all the advantages of marriage, an absence of formal commitment may leave you feeling like something is missing. Realizing you're just "playing house" without setting down permanent roots may become dissatisfying over time.

5. Social and Family Pressures

Friends and family may constantly question why you haven't tied the knot, creating added strain in your relationship. Explaining to others your decision to still be in a rental property relationship can be tiring, especially if they don't respect or understand why this choice has been made.

6. Uncertainty About the Future

Without an obvious way forward, it's easy to become hopelessly stuck. Without knowing where the relationship stands or its final goal, time spent investing could easily go to waste if there is no endgame in sight.

The Issue: Without knowing the next steps ahead of you, it can be easy to feel lost. Whether or not your efforts have paid off will depend heavily on whether a clear path forward exists for both of you.

Why It Is Difficult: Spending years investing yourself could end up making you regretful years later. On reflection it might leave one wondering whether the relationship was a worthwhile investment of time spent.

Should You Date a Rental Property? Who Is It Best Suited For:

Women who don't prioritize marriage or value flexibility in their relationships can find great success dating rental property owners; in particular, those who are content with a partnership without the legal and social obligations that come with traditional unions.

* Independent women who enjoy shared experiences without formal commitments should continue cautiously, women who view marriage as essential to forming lasting relationships should go ahead carefully and invest emotionally before making their choice.

* Women experiencing long-term uncertainty or misaligned goals.

Final Thought on Mr. Rent-to-Own

Mr. Rent-to-Own provides something truly rare in modern dating: an opportunity to explore commitment without feeling pressured into making hasty commitment decisions. While he may not yet be your Forever Home, Mr. RTO gives you ample time and space to decide if this relationship has enough substance for a lasting future together.

But here's the key: while Mr. Rent-to-Own may seem like an appealing solution for many people, it only works if both parties involved are clear about their goals and act with integrity when communicating with each other. If someone seems disinterested or you begin second-guessing the arrangement, it may be best to leave sooner rather than later.

So, if you're ready to explore the idea of forever without jumping headfirst, Mr. Rent-to-Own could be just what's needed for you. Take your time assessing a deal before making your move, whether that is this property or another. Your forever home awaits!

Rent-to-Own: Like Dating a Rent-A-Center

When I think of rent-to-own, all I can picture is a place like Rent-A-Center. Sure, you can own it at the end, but baby, by the time you get there, you've *definitely* paid for it—and then some! (This is my opinion)

It's like getting that sofa on a payment plan. At first, it seems manageable, even exciting. But as the months roll on, you realize you've paid triple the sticker price, and now you're wondering if that couch was really worth it.

Same with relationships. Rent-to-own sounds great in theory—testing the waters, taking your time—but just make sure that by the time you "own" it, you haven't spent so much that you're too exhausted to enjoy it. Because honey, love shouldn't come with hidden fees and balloon payments!

CHAPTER 5

Hold on tight, ladies: this next property may cost you everything.

Mr. Money Pit will drain your emotional reserves while draining away finances - leaving you sitting on your parents' couch with an insufficient bank balance, damaged credit score, and a standing appointment with a therapist - welcome to Mr. Money Pit's world: it comes complete with warning labels warning of impending bankruptcies of both heart and wallet!

Cancerians with big hearts like me know this all too well: wanting to believe the best in people and see potential where others see problems. Unfortunately, though, I know first-hand there is a difference between being someone's kind partner and becoming their personal ATM; unfortunately, Mr. Money Pit doesn't just dip his hand into your finances--he dives right in, leaving behind overdraft fees and regret.

Meet Mr. Money Pit! This charming yet dangerously charming individual will pull at your heartstrings with puppy-dog eyes and an emotional story you just can't ignore: his car just broke down, so he needs some cash to fix it; in return, he offers you a project which promises triple returns; yet somehow, each time you look around he, wants more money.

Dating Mr. Money Pit can be both emotionally and financially draining. Not only is he asking for your money; he's asking for your trust, faith, and belief in his potential. When he tells you, "This is for us, baby," your instinctual reaction may be to believe him despite any risk to yourself or to his character.

Why Mr. Money Pit Is So Dangerous

1. Financial Drain

What happens: Your finances quickly drain away as you find yourself giving him every crisis or co-signing loans you will likely never repay.

Why It Is Difficult: The financial toll doesn't just hit your wallet; it has an effect on both your peace of mind and ability to plan for the future.

2. Emotional Manipulation

What Is Happening: He employs guilt, charm, and promises an improved future as emotional manipulation techniques to keep you hooked on their plan.

Why It Is Difficult: Because your feelings start to fluctuate between wanting to help and protecting yourself.

3. Never-Ending Issues

Just when you think he's turned a corner, something else arises-- whether it be his car, job, or family matters--stamping down any progress being made toward his future success or simply their "big break."

Why it is Difficult: Feeling powerless over his decisions to put out his money and energy.

4. Strained Relationships

It's what happens: As time passes, your friends and family become aware of its impact on you and may try to intervene to try and help him.

Why it is difficult: Advocating for him--or hiding the truth about him--may cause irreparable damage in relationships you care deeply about.

Red Flags to Watch Out for

* Recurring Stories Requiring Funds: Every time you turn around, there's another financial emergency needing your support.

* Big Promises Without Delivery of Results

He makes big promises, but the results never materialize.

* Emotional Guilt Trips: He takes advantage of your sympathy to make you feel guilty if you say no.

No Evidence of Change: Even after helping him, nothing changes due to him depending on you instead of taking responsibility for himself and finding solutions on his own.

1. Set Clear Boundaries

To avoid becoming the bank of someone's financial burdens, set up clear boundaries.

2. Stop Funding His Lifestyle

If he truly needs help, encourage him to seek professional financial advice or help--not you.

3. Focus On Actions, Not Words

Pay attention to whether he's actively taking steps to improve his situation or just making excuses.

4. Prioritize Your Own Needs

Protect both your financial and emotional well-being; remember, however, that you're not the one tasked with fixing him.

The Hard Truth About Mr. Money Pit

Mr. Money Pit can be more than a financial drain; he can also sap your spirit. Love doesn't require giving up your own stability for someone else's needs, and being an excellent partner doesn't involve taking care of all their issues at once. At its core, healthy relationships should feel like investments that contribute to your happiness rather than liabilities. If your relationship leaves you constantly broken financially or emotionally, it might be time for a reevaluation - even though there may be potential in "Mr. Money Pit," it isn't up to you alone to build him back from scratch.

Why Women Who Are Mentally Broken or Overly Trusting Are Susceptible to the Money Pit

It can be easy for those in vulnerable states - be they mental, emotional, or financial - to fall for Mr. Money Pit, especially women who are already emotionally broken or overly trusting. His charming presence can easily draw them in; after all he knows how to appeal to your nurturing side. Let's consider why such relationships may appeal particularly to these types of women:

Need for Appreciation

If you are feeling emotionally fragile, helping another can give you a sense of purpose and self-worth.

> * **Why it Happens:** Mr. Money Pit has a gift for manipulating you into believing they need you and that only you can save them from their dire situations. He plays into your need to feel important, loved, and indispensable by convincing you they

need help from you - thus playing into their hands and playing into their game plan to manipulate you into believing they need you as their savior.

* **The outcome:** You invest your energy in helping him resolve his issues because it feels like helping yourself at the same time.

Women with a history of over-giving may find themselves drawn to Mr. Money Pit.

* **Why it happens:** If you are used to taking on roles of helping and fixing relationships, Mr. Money Pit's endless crises may feel familiar, and you could misinterpret his dependence as love.

* **The result:** You find yourself trapped in an endless cycle of giving, hoping that eventually your sacrifices will pay off in terms of gratitude, devotion, or love from others.

Low Self-Worth

It can be easy for those suffering mental illness to believe that they don't deserve better or that their worth depends on what they can contribute towards society.

* **Why it happens:** Being relied upon can temporarily boost your self-esteem; but in reality, you might feel unworthy of having a healthier and fairer relationship.

* As a result, they stay in an emotionally draining relationship for fear that nothing better might not present itself.

Helping Others Can Give the Illusion of Control

Giving help can give us an illusion of control when our lives feel out of whack or chaotic.

* **Why it Happens:** By "fixing" Mr. Money Pit's problems, you give yourself the illusion that progress has been made--both for him and yourself. Focusing on Mr. Money Pit makes it easier for you to put off confronting any personal pain or insecurities than facing them head-on.

* As a result, you lose sight of your needs and goals, becoming more invested in his life than your own.

Belief in Potential Women who trust often see the best in others, even when all evidence shows otherwise.

* **Why it occurs:** Mr. Money Pit has an incredible knack for selling potential. He promises that this loan, favor, or sacrifice will be "the one" that transforms everything, making you believe his promises and not their reality.

* **As a result,** you stay longer than necessary, hoping he will keep promises that never materialize. When your mind has become irreparably damaged, contemplating being alone can feel unbearable.

* **Why it happens:** Mr. Money Pit offers companionship - even if it is conditional or manipulative. He fills an emotional void, so leaving means losing both partner and sense of connection.

* **The result**: Clinging on even when the relationship is clearly harming you

1. **Recognize Your Patterns**: Recognizing patterns is the first step toward change; do not discount their effect. Awareness is your ticket out.

2. **Rebuilding Your Self-Worth**: Concentrate on healing and personal growth for yourself. Surround yourself with people who uphold you and remind you of your value.

3. **Setting Boundaries:** Discover ways of saying no without guilt to protect both finances and emotional energy.

4. **Seek Support:** Speaking to a therapist or trusted friend can be helpful in working through any negative emotions surrounding Mr. Money Pit.

5. **Focus on Your Goals**: Instead of fixing him, try shifting your attention towards creating a life that fulfills you instead.

Final Thought on Mr. Money Pit

Mr. Money Pit exploits your vulnerabilities, but that doesn't make you weak for being drawn in by him. Instead, it shows that you care deeply and have generous hearts - however, excessive generosity without boundaries can become self-destructive. It is essential that you understand your worth as an individual and recognize that true love doesn't come at the expense of financial stability or emotional wellbeing.

So, if you find yourself trapped in an unhealthy relationship with Mr. Money Pit, remember you deserve a partner who lifts rather than breaks you down. Break free, rebuild yourself, and trust that someone strong and caring like yourself exists out there waiting to find them.

Sometimes the best thing you can do for yourself and him is simply walk away. Let Mr. Money Pit sort out his foundation while you focus on finding an asset (and partner) that adds more value than detracts. Remember, your worth isn't decided by how much you give, but by how well you protect your peace and prioritize happiness in yourself and others.

So, if you find yourself with a Money Pit property, ask yourself whether the investment is worthwhile or whether now may be the time to cut your losses and move forward with life.

Ladies: Save Your Coins and Avoid the Money Pit

Listen up, ladies: save your coins and ditch that Money Pit! We don't want you to become so frustrated over being played that you try plotting revenge... only to realize there's no bail money available due to him draining all your resources dry!

* **Why it happens**: If you are used to taking on roles of helping and fixing relationships, Mr. Money Pit's endless crises may feel familiar, and you could misinterpret his dependence as love.

* **The result:** You find yourself trapped in an endless cycle of giving, hoping that eventually your sacrifices will pay off in terms of gratitude, devotion, or love from others.

Hey Ladies! Take a Breather--We Haven't Even Reached Half!

Phew! I know I have provided plenty of things to consider today, but do not rush off and fold your cards just yet: this journey has only begun. Who could have predicted that taking on real estate could teach us so much about navigating our relationship game?

But here's the thing: while most people around us are playing checkers, we are learning Monopoly! That means it is all about strategy instead of chance - deeds, investments, knowing when to pass "Go," and most importantly of all, knowing when it is best to kick Mr. Money Pit off the board are all part of playing successfully at this game.

Before we jump back in, let's pause for a brief stretch and release tension from our relationships that seem destined for nothingness. Take a sip of water (or wine! I won't judge) and get ready to elevate your love life even more.

Because trust me, ladies, there is more for you to discover than meets the eye. Properties become trickier, stakes increase, and lessons become deeper--but don't fret; by the end of it all, you will emerge with an extensive portfolio and heart full of green.

Are you ready to keep going? Let's throw the dice and see what lies in store!

CHAPTER 6

◆ ◆ ◆

Okay ladies, let me introduce you to Mr. Fixer Upper

Now we all understand what the Money Pit is--an immense mess you must leave just where it was found. But there's another type of man often confused with Mr. Money Pit, and I am here to clarify his identity and distinctions.

This next property has tremendous promise. Mr. Fixer Upper doesn't expect charity; he needs someone to recognize the diamond in the rough and help bring out its fullest potential. With the right partner and some TLC--not necessarily financial investment--this individual could transform from "meh" to "wow!"

Why Mr. Fixer Upper Isn't Just Another Money Pit

Mr. Fixer Upper, unlike its more irresponsible counterpart, Mr. Money Pit, is focused on growth. While you might not see him as "Mr. Perfect," there is potential in him - whether it's emotional growth or strengthening foundational structures; Mr. Fixer Upper can become something amazing with proper nurturing and effort.

Pros and Cons of Dating Mr. Fixer Upper

The Benefits:

* **A Lower Initial Investment:** He may not instantly fall under

your spell, but the potential returns could make him worth investing in

* **Customizability:** You can help mold him into someone that better aligns with your values and goals over time.

* **Shared Journey:** Contributing together toward building something significant can strengthen and deepen your bond, with significant equity gains with time and care invested into ensuring Mr. Fixer Upper becomes a relationship of great emotional value that you'll cherish for life.

* **Equity Gain:** If done with care and effort, Mr. Fixer Upper could become something you both hold onto for many years to come!

Cons:

There may be negative repercussions associated with being together during construction efforts that may hinder progress.

* **Time Commitment**: Renovations need time and patience, just like personal growth does.

* **Emotional Labor:** Supporting someone can take effort on both ends; otherwise, it quickly becomes one-sided and could become counterproductive.

* **Uncertainty:** Not every Fixer Upper becomes your dream home; there is always the risk that they don't meet their full potential.

* **Stressful Renovations:** Growth can be challenging, leading to miscommunications, setbacks, and growing pains which all need to be managed along the way.

   1. **Is He Willing to Put in the Work?** Remember faith without work is dead.

   2. **Do They Have Strong Foundations?** Underneath his flaws, is he kind, supportive and respectful? A Fixer Upper

with solid foundation should be worth exploring further.

3. **Are You Up for the Process?** Renovating relationships requires patience and resilience; if this task proves too challenging for you to manage it may be best left behind.

When to Leave Mr. Fixer Upper: Knowing When It Isn't Worth the Investment

Sometimes no matter how much potential or effort we invest, Mr. Fixer Upper turns out to be more of a hassle than an asset. Renovating relationships is always rewarding when both partners are dedicated to the process, when repairs pile up without progress being made then perhaps it is time for both of you to step back and reassess.

1. **He's Not Doing His Part**

In a successful partnership, both partners should actively be working to improve the relationship and themselves.

* **What It Means**: You are continually encouraging, supporting, and making sacrifices, but his behavior is still, unchanged--or worse still reversed.

* **Why it is a dealbreaker:** If you are the sole person putting in work on renovation, which doesn't constitute partnership--it's more like running your own one-woman renovation show.

2. **His "Foundation" Is Lackluster**

Fixer Uppers come with strong bones--kindness, respect, ambition--but others cannot be restored.

* **What it looks like:** He acts dishonestly, disrespectfully, or lacks essential traits such as empathy or accountability.

* **Why it is a dealbreaker:** Living in a house with a crumbling foundation is unsafe no matter what renovations have been

completed on it; similarly, relationships that lack trust and respect cannot thrive for long.

3 The Renovations Are Never-Ending

Every relationship faces difficulties, but when issues don't diminish over time it may be time to part ways.

* **What it looks like:** Every time, you solve one problem, two more appear, and you are tired from constantly trying to "fix" things.

* **Why it is a Dealbreaker:** If the relationship feels like an endless money pit of emotional labor, it may no longer be sustainable--or fair for you.

4. He Refuses Change

Change needs effort on both parties involved, but some individuals just may not want or be ready to commit.

* **What It Looks Like:** He disregards your concerns, blames others for his problems, or refuses to take responsibility for his actions.

* **Why It Is a Dealbreaker:** Without taking responsibility for his own growth and nurturing their development, he won't progress any time soon, despite your best efforts or patience on your part.

5. You Are Losing Yourself

Supporting someone else's growth shouldn't come at the cost of your happiness, goals, or self-worth.

* **What it looks like:** Consistently prioritizing his needs over yours to the point that you feel drained, unfulfilled, or like an impostor of yourself.

* **Why It Is a Dealbreaker:** Healthy relationships should

enhance rather than diminish your life; if a significant sacrifice has to be made for one to exist; it might be time for reconsideration of that particular connection.

6. Are You Waiting for "Someday" That Never Comes?

Fixer Uppers have the potential to become Mr. Right if they actively pursue that transformation.

* **What it looks like:** He keeps promising to change "someday," yet there is no evidence he is taking steps in that direction.

* **Why It Is a Dealbreaker**: "Someday" is no guarantee, and you deserve someone who shows up and makes progress at once.

7. Return on Investment Is Not Enough

Relationship need effort, but should also bring joy, support, and love in return. If none of those benefits exist for you it could be time for change.

* **What it looks like**: Feeling more exhausted than uplifted, frustrated than fulfilled

***Why it should be a dealbreaker**: You deserve a partner who contributes positively to your happiness, not someone who takes without giving anything in return.

Going Through with Break-up Decisions

Breaking up is never an easy decision to make, especially when we have invested our time, energy, and emotions into a relationship. Sometimes, though, no matter what their potential, there comes a moment when reality sets in: They just aren't prepared or capable enough of becoming the partner you deserve. Let's examine more closely why it may be time for a breakup as well as ways we can navigate it with grace and confidence.

Understand Reality

Acknowledging that no amount of effort will change a person who does not wish to change is key in setting healthy boundaries with anyone, including your significant other.

Deliberate Step Back from Relationship

Stepping away can protect both emotional and mental well-being by protecting emotional and mental well-being by setting clear parameters in relation to this relationship.

Put Your Focus Where It Should Be

Put all your energy and attention on yourself for personal development and happiness.

Let Go of Guilt: Stepping away doesn't signify failure - rather, it shows that you prioritized yourself first.

Be Open to New Opportunities: Breaking away from Mr. Fixer Upper allows space for someone more suitable. Unfortunately, we often stick around longer than necessary because of his potential, or since we have invested significant time and energy into him.

* **You fear giving up on someone important.** Oftentimes we are trying to save the relationship because we are keeping the faith that the frog will turn into a Prince.

* **You fear you won't find anyone better.** These feelings are valid; however, staying out of guilt, fear, or hope that he'll change will only prolong your unhappiness and increase its

intensity.

Acknowledge Your Effort

Acknowledging your efforts doesn't indicate failure; instead, it means accepting that you have reached your limits and walking away gracefully is sometimes necessary.

Communicate Clearly

Once you've decided it's time to part ways, have an honest dialogue about why. Explain your reasons clearly, but do not try to justify yourself further than necessary.

Set up Boundaries

Once you leave, set firm boundaries to avoid being drawn back into the cycle and backslidden again. This might involve stopping communication or cutting off contact altogether until both of you have had time to heal and move on with your lives.

Concentrate on Your Growth

Get back into focusing on yourself. Set and pursue goals, practice self-care, and surround yourself with supportive people who encourage you.

Forgive Yourself

It is natural to experience mixed feelings during times of change--sadness, guilt, and even anger--but these should not define who you are. Give yourself time to work through them while remembering how strong it was to break free and move forward with life after. Celebrate any strength it took for you to walk away!

Not Every Fixer Upper Is Worth the Risk

Not all Fixer Uppers are bad investments. If he's actively improving himself, accepting feedback, and committed to their relationship, then there may be potential for growth; but if the relationship causes more harm than good, then perhaps it is time for parting ways.

Mr. Fixer Upper can become your perfect partner with the right partner and mutual effort, providing him with an opportunity to flourish into someone truly remarkable. Don't simply look at love as "fixing" someone; rather, it should support each person's individual growth while at the same time nurturing your own. If Mr. Fixer Upper is willing to meet you halfway and put forth effort, then maybe just possibly, you might discover someone that fulfills all your hopes and expectations--plus more.

Ladies, if you have the patience and vision, don't overlook this diamond in the rough. However, if he seems more interested in becoming your full-time renovation crew than in contributing positively to your life. Send him back out onto the market. Mr. Fixer Upper can either become an inspiring success story or an expensive mistake, depending on whether he's willing to put in the necessary work, which ultimately determines whether it adds or subtracts from your life.

At the end of the day, you're not just an employee--you're also a partner! And you deserve someone who is ready to collaborate with you and share in building your life together - not someone who expects you to shoulder all the weight alone. So, when contemplating whether to stay or go ask yourself this: am I creating my future here or just patching holes in someone else's foundation? If it is the latter then walk away; your time, energy, and love are worth far more than any Fixer-Upper who doesn't respect or value your contributions as individuals.

Ladies! Take a Deep Breath...

That was quite a revelation, no doubt! Now you may be sitting quietly, sipping coffee (or wine), looking at your man out of the corner of your eye and thinking to yourself, "Didn't they just ask to borrow $40 last week?"

Listen, I don't intend to raise any controversy, just a bit. But here's the thing: I'm not raising red flags to ruin your day--instead, these are things I wish someone had told me before I ended up mired in overdraft fees and emotional exhaustion.

If he seems solid, don't worry; however, if his features resemble those described as Money Pit or Fixer Upper we may need to discuss further. Take a deep breath, side-eye him once more for good measure, and let's keep this journey moving along - trust me; we're just getting into the good stuff now.

CHAPTER 7

Ladies, Are you a member of a Church? -This next property will have You at the Altar Praying

Be ready, ladies: this man may make you consider joining a church! His presence will have you lighting candles, singing hymns, and asking God for guidance in every aspect of life.

Let's be real--women are resilient when it comes to heartbreak, while men can take years after being rejected by an elementary school crush to heal from their heartache and move on with life. It is a mystery for all time; and we all have known someone like this - an ex-wife, girlfriend, or baby mama has left him vulnerable with trust issues, emotional baggage, and mental scars which keep coming up time after time!

Meet Mr. Foreclosure - your friendly neighborhood foreclosure!

Mr. Foreclosure: Damaged But Discounted

This man resembles a foreclosed home: full of potential yet damaged from past relationships that left him battered, bruised, and perhaps missing some "appliances," including even his dishwasher (his ex-took that!). While underneath all that lies a good person who deserves better, some time and care must be invested before fully functioning as a partner again.

Pros and Cons of Dating Mr. Foreclosure

The Benefits:

* **Potential for Growth**: If given proper care and commitment, Mr. Foreclosure can become a great partner.

* **Customizable Relationship**: By working together, you have an opportunity to tailor the relationship exactly as it suits your needs.

* **Motivated to Settle**: Once wounded, people tend to seek someone who understands them without playing games or engaging in toxic relationships.

The Cons:

* **Emotional Repairs Needed:** Following past traumas, rebuilding trust will take time, effort, and patience from both sides.

* **Trust Issues**: His past may make him skeptical or unwilling to open up completely.

* **Renovation Stresses**: Helping someone heal may be emotionally taxing, especially if he has not engaged in self-work.

* **Unpredictable Condition:** He may not even realize how damaged his body is, leading to miscommunication or conflicts between themselves and their loved ones.

How Can I Know If Mr. Foreclosure Is Worth It?

1. **Check His Foundation:** Are they willing to grow and heal?
2. **Evaluate Your Patience:** Are you prepared to put in time and emotional energy towards rebuilding trust?

3. **Recognize Your Limits:** If someone stays stuck in their past or refuses to move forward with life, don't make their past damage your burden.

Ladies, be wary. While Mr. Foreclosure can be an attractive prospect, don't become their sole rehabilitation team. If the two of you can't meet halfway in terms of meeting up halfway and building healthy relationships together, it is impossible when one partner still lives in their past.

Before embarking on any DIY project, ask yourself this question: Am I equipped with the necessary tools, time, and patience for this endeavor? If you don't, don't sweat it! There are plenty of homes - and men! - on the market waiting to welcome someone just like you into their homes.

Sometimes Mr. Foreclosure's potential isn't enough to sustain your belief, no matter how hard you try. His past may be holding him and you back; although leaving someone who's hurt you can be difficult, but staying in a relationship that drains emotionally or mentally from you is never the right option - here's how you can tell when and how best to move on gracefully.

He's Bogged Down by His Past

If Mr. Foreclosure keeps going back over past hurts or harbors resentment towards an ex, that should be taken as a red flag.

Symptoms could include him often bringing up their ex and placing blame or making comparisons to her instead of you as evidence.

Why it is a dealbreaker: No relationship can thrive when one partner stays mired in their past. If he can't see beyond it, he isn't right for you either.

He's Not Willing to Heal

Healing takes effort, so your partner must be open to engaging in it himself rather than expecting you to fix him.

What this looks like: He declines therapy sessions or avoids difficult conversations; or denies having trust issues altogether.

Why It Is a Dealbreaker: Although you can provide support to aid someone's healing, ultimately, they must do the work themselves; otherwise, you may end up carrying the relationship yourself and carrying the damage with them. (Third Party Damage).

If his trust issues, emotional baggage, or unresolved pain are having an impact on your mental wellbeing, then now may be the time for a reevaluation.

What this looks like: He acts suspiciously towards you emotionally or takes out his anger on you directly.

Reasons why it should be a dealbreaker: Relationships should enrich our lives rather than take from them, so if someone's baggage is hindering that growth, it might be time for parting ways.

Repairs Seem Endless

Sometimes no matter how much effort is put into the relationship, nothing changes despite your best efforts. That may include communicating, compromising, and even suggesting therapy sessions, but nothing seems to change for either party involved.

Why it is a dealbreaker: If the relationship feels like an endless renovation with no tangible benefits, it may not be worth your while and energy to pursue further.

You Are Losing Yourself

If the relationship requires sacrificing your happiness, goals, or identity in exchange for its survival, it's time to leave.

What it Looks Like: No longer Pursuing Passions | Feel Constantly Drained | Don't Recognize Whom

Why this is a dealbreaker: For healthy relationships to thrive, they must allow room for both of you to develop as individuals without hindering or restricting it.

Steps You Can Take!

Be Honest with Yourself

Understand that love or effort alone won't change someone who's unwilling to change, which is the first step toward breaking free of an unhelpful situation.

Hold Direct Conversations

Sit him down and explain your feelings calmly and clearly, including why the relationship no longer suits your needs and why you have decided to move on from it.

What to Say: "I care for you, but your past is keeping us from forging a healthy future together. I need to put myself first."

Set Boundaries

Once separated, create space to heal by setting boundaries on communication and not allowing your ex to pressure or coerce you back together.

Seek Support

Discuss your decision with close family, friends, and/or therapists who can support and reassure you. Be surrounded by individuals who provide comfort and encouragement.

Focus on Your Future

Reconnect with yourself by rediscovering passions and setting new goals; reminding yourself that a relationship based on mutual trust and respect deserves your consideration. Let's face it--trying to help heal another foreclosure while simultaneously dealing with your own is impossible! Being involved in both situations is like two sinking ships trying to save each other at the same time: everybody ends up wet in the end.

Healing can be challenging enough; when combined with someone else's baggage, it becomes a much larger undertaking than expected. Instead of finding strength together and building something beautiful together, your relationship could easily end up as an albatross around both of your necks.

Before trying to flip someone else's "property," make sure your own foundation is solid first. Otherwise, both parties involved could end up facing foreclosure simultaneously; heal yourself first before trying to find someone with whom you can co-build a dream home together.

Dating someone facing foreclosure shouldn't be about saving them; rather, it should be about finding someone willing to partner in rebuilding their lives. A healthy relationship requires mutual effort, trust, and forming shared goals for the future.

Before investing in a foreclosure property, ask yourself these three questions:

* Is he making real attempts to grow?

* Am I receiving enough support from this relationship?

* Do I envision a future with him that adds to, rather than detracts from, my life?

If the answer to both these questions is "yes," go ahead but, set boundaries on the relationship; otherwise, don't be afraid to walk away - prioritizing your healing and happiness should come first!

F inal Thought on Mr. Foreclosure
Remember, you aren't an administrator, therapist, or savior; you are their partner. Helping someone progress may be satisfying, but only if both parties contribute equal effort in working toward that end.

Imagine this: while passing by an attractive house with great curb appeal and sparkling windows, your mind wanders down a path toward its potential as your dream home - only to open its door and find that everything has been stripped bare - no walls, no floors, no appliances - not even a sink to cry into.

Once you find an ideal house at an incredible price, renovation costs quickly add up and now occupy all your time and energy to make it livable. Looking at all your bills and torn drywall leaves one wondering: "Should I have just waited for one that was move-in ready?"

But here's the challenge: with plenty of love, patience, and perseverance, this Foreclosure could become your forever home! Mr. Foreclosure can often yield huge returns; just make sure you can manage the chaos before signing that dotted line!

CHAPTER 8

Ladies, Brace Up--It's Going to Get Bumpy!

Alright, ladies, buckle your seatbelts because this ride may get bumpy. I hope that everyone ate before entering, as I don't want anyone getting carsick when we meet our next type of man - one who should have been cast in The Fast and the Furious as he races towards his altar with all cylinders revved up!

Men, too, have their own biological clock. Once their clock starts ticking, men don't waste any time acting upon it. In some cases, "we met at a gas station on Monday and by Wednesday they are tagging you in their Facebook relationship status update!" levels of speed. Still need convincing? Consider this scenario: you meet him on Thanksgiving and by Christmas he has invited you to meet his mother - without even an informal introduction - she already wants you to wear something appropriate to their upcoming wedding - yet you still don't know his last name!

These men seem eager to find someone fast, almost like they're searching for a green card. Sure, marriage can be beautiful when done for the right reasons, but offer lifelong commitment in as little as seven days? That isn't romance--that is desperation for a wife right away.

Why the Haste? Honestly, no one knows. Even if wedding magazines line your coffee table (as that may be part of your business), this kind of rush can feel more like high-pressure sales pitches than love itself.

Ladies, meet Mr. Short Sale! His interest lies in quick transactions, but don't let his urgency deceive you--this is your life, not a fire sale! Take your time deciding and planning before accepting his offer on terms that suit you - not his clock ticking away. Now is a good time to slow down, take a deep breath, and decide whether this vehicle is indeed your ride - or whether it may be time to opt out of highway travel altogether.

Dating a Short Sale: An Adrenaline Rush

Dating a Short Sale can be like entering into a roller coaster ride of commitment. Mr. Short Sale doesn't come around just to "see where things go," he's already plotted out your future together and takes swift steps to secure things as soon as he meets you; from changing his relationship status on Facebook after two dates to meeting up with his mom at Thanksgiving leftovers, Mr. Short Sale is on a mission!

At first, his enthusiasm may seem exciting, but quickly becomes tiring or even uncomfortable. While it might appear to be the solution to your romantic woes, hidden costs and potential pitfalls in this relationship dynamic may be worth exploring further.

What It's Like Dating a Short Sale?

He Moves Fast--Really Fast

Your relationship will move at a breakneck speed; from exchanging numbers to talking about future children in record time. Every milestone, from dates, exclusivity agreements, and family meets to potential engagement will pass quickly by.

He's Persistent and Charming

Mr. Short Sale knows exactly how to make you feel special: attentive, communicative, and enthusiastic in his intentions for you as the center of his world. But his insistence may prove too much if you aren't yet comfortable with his pace and pace-setting ways.

His Quick Moves Feel Forced

Although his advances may appear romantic, they could also come off as intrusive and pressurize you into feeling as if he loves just being part of your relationship.

He Needs Stability-Fast

A Short Sale often experiences heartbreak, financial hardships, or personal challenges, which require him to find someone to help rebuild himself quickly.

Pros of Dating a Short Sale

1. It's unlike guys who waste your time, Mr. Short Sale is clear about his goals and is unafraid of going after them.
2. No Games, No Guesswork
3. He Communicates His Intent Clearly

His eagerness often comes with grand displays of affection--flowers, love notes, and declarations that make you feel genuinely loved.

4. Accelerated Milestones

If you're ready for commitment, his pace can feel rejuvenating, ending the endless wait that often characterizes modern dating.

5. Security

If stability is what you seek, his desire to tie things down may give you peace of mind and feel safe and wanted.

Cons of Dating a Short Sale

His Urgency Can Feel Overwhelming

His urgency may pressure you into making decisions before you are comfortable doing so, which could result in feelings of pressure or regret later.

Lack of Genuine Connection

Moving too quickly doesn't always allow for the deep emotional bonding necessary for a healthy relationship, or expose hidden issues which might drive his haste in making commitment decisions, such as loneliness, insecurity, or fear of being alone-- not true compatibility.

Emotional Burnout

Mentally, you will not know if you are coming or going. Being emotionally drained is not sexy at all!

His Pursuit Can Be Exhausting

The intensity of his pursuit may leave you exhausted, leaving your emotions spinning out of control.

You May Overlook Red Flags

A relationship's swift progress may make it more difficult for you to identify potential red flags or incompatibilities early enough.

When to Embark upon Mr. Short Sale: If you're ready for commitment and don't wish to waste any more time looking, Mr. Short Sale's directness could be refreshing in its approach.

When to Leave Mr. Short Sale!

If Feeling Pressurized

If his urgency makes you uncomfortable or rushes you through activities, or if the relationship moves too fast for comfort, that could be a telltale sign that the relationship might not be progressing properly.

He Projects His Needs on You

If it seems as though he's more focused on filling an emotional void in his life rather than creating genuine connections with you, it might be time for an evaluation.

Your Timelines Don't Align

If a man doesn't meet your timeline for commitment, don't feel pressured into agreeing at once - take your time finding something more compatible! If his haste puts off dating someone like yourself, it is okay to say no and find someone more fitting of your goals and timeline.

Rushing into a relationship should never be done on impulse; otherwise, it can pose safety concerns that should not be ignored. Without enough time to fully get to know someone, you are more likely vulnerable to manipulation or ulterior agendas from other people in your new romantic partnership.

Lack of Knowledge on His Background

Beginning any relationship without fully understanding their history, values, and intentions can leave you vulnerable. If they're pressuring for rapid commitment, ask yourself why and consider whether this would help both of you or just him.

Potential for Control

Fast-moving relationships may sometimes mask possessive or controlling behaviors. If he tries to isolate you from friends, rush major life decisions onto you quickly, or demand constant attention, then this should be seen as red flags that should not be ignored.

Loss of Personal Boundaries

It can be challenging to keep personal boundaries during an intensely romantic relationship. If he's insistent on merging finances or moving in together early on, or making other significant life-altering decisions without first consulting you first, take a step back and reevaluate before acting impulsively.

A successful relationship isn't built quickly--it takes time, trust, respect, and understanding for it to thrive. While Mr. Short Sale may seem charming at first, don't allow his enthusiasm to cloud your judgment; take your time in making this critical decision and pose challenging questions to ensure you enter an environment that meets both of your values.

Final Thoughts on Mr. Short Sale

Diving headlong into relationships may feel thrilling, but love is a journey, not a race. A genuine partnership takes time to form through patience, trust, and effort from both parties involved. If Mr. Short Sale is genuine, he'll respect your need to move at a pace that feels right to you, and if not, take time to assess whether a relationship built to last exists before diving in headfirst.

Because relationships that last are not about speed but about stability. A true partner will take time and care in building yours without shortcuts or rush jobs being taken. Sis, Grab Your Running Shoes or Fast Car--Speedy Gonzalez Is Coming Fast!

Listen, sister! If you want to deal with Mr. Short Sale successfully, you need to lace up some running shoes or get in your fast car immediately! He moves so fast he's breaking sound barriers: before you know it, he has you walking down an aisle while juggling five children all within two years!

At least give yourself enough time for a background check to come back. (You might learn something.) Mr. Short Sale may offer quick deals quickly; while that might work for some, it might not work as well for everyone.

So, take it slow. Love isn't a race--it's about finding what works for both of you!

Sis, Don't Turn Yourself into a Short Sale Either!

Now let's switch things around--don't become the short sale either! Don't give all your assets away to any man who approaches with an offer like they were the last cupcakes at a bakery - trust me, men find women's short sales just as frightening!

When your prospective partner comes over, try to conceal wedding magazines as contraband and stop scratching that ring finger before he starts thinking you have a rash--or worse, an engagement timeline!

Remember, sis, that you're building your dream home. Take your time, set your terms, and make sure that he deserves to enter before planning the honeymoon. Are You hydrated, Sis? Have you grabbed your drink yet, Sis--we're about to dive into the drama!

CHAPTER 9

Did You Grab Your Wine, Coffee, Tea, or Bottled Water Yet?

After this emotional "Waiting to Exhale" type reading experience, honey, your body needs water to remain hydrated in preparation for what comes next.

Take a deep breath because this next man may leave you reeling! He may leave you questioning your sanity, searching online for ways to survive being Sister Wives. He could very well be that person; someone who makes you wonder if you're the only one or merely his latest "commitment."

Start saving your pearls, as this chapter promises to deliver some stunning revelations! Get ready for an emotional rollercoaster of an experience!

Ladies, Meet Mr. Bank-Owned Property--Where Mama holds the deed. Let me just start off by saying this--I have two sons whom I adore deeply: they're my babies, my heartbeats, my everything. They will never grow away from my love (Mama bears understand!). But I recognize there are boundaries that shouldn't be crossed, regardless of our affection for our kids.

What Is Mr. Bank-Owned Property?

A person known as Mr. Bank-Owned Property may still rely on his or her mother as the deed holder for all decisions made and moves planned, opinions aired, and plans put into action - all decisions, moves, and opinions all pass through his mother, known as his banker (Mama). Want to plan a vacation? Better check with Mom first.

Looking forward to hosting Thanksgiving at your place this year? No one should forget that the banker must always be the center of attention on special holidays! If you plan on surprising him with something new for Thanksgiving dinner, "That's not how Mama makes it!" should come as an answer. Welcome to Sister Wives: Mother-Son Edition.

If His Mother Doesn't Approve--Run for the Hills

Let me warn you: if Mama doesn't approve of you, game over! These mothers don't just disapprove quietly - they sabotage, manipulate, and guilt trip like professionals.

* **Guilt as a Weapon**: "I sacrificed so much for you, and this is how you repay me?"

* **Sabotage Moves:** If she senses you may not be "good enough," she may try to undermine your relationship, create drama, or persuade him you don't belong in his life.

* **Comparisons Are Ever present**: If your cooking, cleaning, or nurturing doesn't measure up to hers, he will let you know it immediately "Mama's dish was better." This behavior could last all your life!

Pros and Cons of Mr. Bank-Owned Property

1. **Family-Oriented:** He places immense value on family life, which can make him an excellent partner when balanced properly.

2. **Attentive and Nurturing:** Growing up with a nurturing mother figure could give him this quality as well.

3. **Respect for Women**: He's likely been taught respect for women by his mother (assuming healthy boundaries were set).

Unfortunately, her approval can dictate everything from the type of housing available to where you'll live.

4. **No Boundaries**: If the umbilical cord is still metaphorically attached, it will feel as if you're dating both simultaneously.

5. **Guilt Manipulation**: Mama can easily cause guilt trips that will affect not just him but you as well.

6. **Comparison Central**: You are constantly being compared to his mother--her cooking, her cleaning, everything.

How to Handle Mr. Bank-Owned Property

1. **Evaluate Boundaries**: As soon as possible, see his decision-making habits without consulting Mama; can he make them without seeking her approval, or do they rely on her approval instead?

2. **Set Your Expectations**: Be clear about setting healthy boundaries between you and his mother as you set up a life together, respecting both of their relationships as you create new ones together.

3. **Assess Mama's Role**: Take note of whether she dominates or

supports; is she supportive or domineering?

4. Decide What You Can Handle: If the man in question is willing to work on boundaries with you, then perhaps it might be worth exploring further; otherwise, consider whether sharing your relationship with his mother permanently is right.

When to Walk Away
1. **His Mother Doesn't Like You**, If she is actively subverting your relationship, and not standing up for you, it may be time for change.

2. **He Is Bound by Mama** If all decisions need approval from Mama before going ahead with them, it could make your relationship seem less equal and less satisfying as an equal partner.

3. **Your Relationship Has Grown Cluttered** Are you feeling like an interloper in his and Mama's relationship?

Now is the time to assess. What makes a man a Mama's boy, and how can we liberate him (Without Negating Family Inheritance)?

Let's discuss Mama's Boys--men who seem unable to make decisions without first consulting the woman who raised them. While their devotion can initially seem endearing, it quickly turns into an ongoing burden that takes over your life and your schedule.

What defines a Mama's Boy? Let's consider some indicators.

* **He Grew Up Under Her Guidance:** She still holds onto those scissors!

* **His Decisions Reflect Her Approval:** Every decision, from dinner plans to life goals, must meet with Mama's approval before being considered valid.

* **Guilt Is His Superhero:** Her mere words of comforting "I raised you better than this" will send him into retreat like an inexpensive lawn chair.

If you find yourself falling for a Mama's Boy, don't panic, there isn't any need to choose between him and your sanity--or risk having them cut off from the family will. Here is how you can gently liberate him without turning Thanksgiving dinner into an uncomfortable wrestling match.

The Liberation Plan: Engaging Him Without Family Drama

1. Recognize Their Bond

To begin with, don't go after Mama right off the bat; she has been there from day one, and he will likely defend herself quickly if attacked. Instead, acknowledge their bond while subtly reminding him that Mama isn't his only support system.

2. Encourage Independence

Start small: give him permission to make decisions without consulting his mother--whether that means selecting a restaurant or planning an overnight trip--without calling her first! Commemorate his decisions as they increase his confidence.

3. Set Boundaries

Politely! It's important to have an honest but firm conversation about boundaries, letting your son know it's okay to value her opinions, but building life together means making decisions as a team (use "we" language instead of combative or conflictual language to avoid being taken personally by her).

4. Winning Over Mama

To effectively free him, sometimes the key lies in winning Mama over. Show her you respect her role while subtly showing that you can provide care as well. Once she trusts you, she may let go.

5. Provide A Subtle Nudge

If relationships become too close, suggest therapy or personal growth activities to strengthen them and not as criticism of Mama.

When to Raise the White Flag

If he seems unwilling or unable to ease Mama's influence over your relationship, or she is actively undermining it, it could be time for a serious reevaluation. You deserve someone who's 100% in for you - not someone juggling their parent and lover as one entity.

Final Thought on Mr. Bank -Owned Property

Liberating a Mama's Boy doesn't need to be an uphill battle; with love, patience, and the right approach, you can help him balance his affection for both of his mothers with his commitment to you. Just remember you're forging a partnership rather than fighting over custody - so if he's open to change and growth, that's great;

otherwise, it might be best if he stays where he is with his own family drama.

At the end of the day, it's not your goal to raise another Mama's Boy: you want someone with whom to build a life together without strings (or aprons!) attached. There's nothing wrong with men who love and respect their mothers; that's a wonderful quality. However, when that love becomes overbearing or manipulative, it no longer serves its intended purpose and must become healthier for both parties involved.

Dating Mr. Bank-Owned Property can feel like buying a house controlled by the bank; no matter what you invest it, someone else always holds control. If he's willing to set boundaries and show independence for themselves, there might be hope in making your relationship last; otherwise, it might be time to find new property - in any event!

Keep this in mind: love isn't about competition - it's about partnership! No relationship should leave you feeling like an outsider in your own life.

Sis, Let's Keep You Off of the Family Ban List

Sis, hopefully, we won't end up banning you from any family events or worse yet, being forced into wearing matching pajama bottoms with his mother for photo ops (because no one signed up for that).

Remain calm, set reasonable boundaries, and remember you're his partner rather than her subcontractor if possible - making Christmas morning work without turning into an awkward episode of Family Feud can be done!

CHAPTER 10

Ladies, Meet Mr. Mobile Home--The Drifting Dreamer

As I grow older, I appreciate stability more. But let's be honest--there are still those out there who crave excitement, while many women relish in changing up the scene - if that describes you, then this man could just be your cup of tea...or shot of tequila.

Pros of Dating Mr. Mobile Home

1. He Is Always Up for Adventure

Plans that spring up at the last minute can always count on this guy!

2. Adaptable and Flexible (at Least For Now).

He isn't one to let life get him down; instead, he goes with the flow. If you want someone casual who's uncommitted and non-threatening, then this guy's your man. No expectations or long-term plans here--just fun.

3. An Outgoing Free Spirit

His relaxed yet carefree demeanor may be just what's needed if the pressures of traditional relationships have worn you down.

Cons of Dating Mr. Mobile Home

1. No Stability

He might seem exciting at first, but where will he build a foundation?

2. Commitment Issues

3. He Can't Settle Down

It may be easier for him to set himself up with one address, but that won't help them settle into relationships as easily.

4. He Brings Along a Lot of Stuff

His life might fit into just two duffel bags- and you may end up carrying some of it too!

5. You Are His Anchor

While his free spirit may be charming, it often shows an insecure state in his life, requiring someone else to provide support he lacks--something which can become increasingly draining over time.

How and When to Let Mr. Mobile Home Go

Dating Mr. Mobile Home can be an exhilarating adventure filled with spontaneity and fun, but eventually its excitement may fade when you realize his nomadic lifestyle doesn't meet your need for stability. Knowing when to let go can save you emotional exhaustion while keeping the door open to finding someone more compatible with your goals.

1. He Refuses to Settle Down

2. If he continues bouncing between his boy's couch and his parents' basement, this could be an indicator that he's not ready to commit fully--including you.

3. You Are Exhausted from Carrying the Load

If it seems as if you are shouldering all the burden and providing all the stability for the relationship, it might be time for some adjustments - a healthy partnership requires balance.

4. Your Goals Don't Align

5. Your Dreams Differ from His

If your goals for building a life together don't mesh with his desires for his next move, it is clear you are both on two very separate tracks.

6. He Is Not Growing or Evolving

Everyone deserves time to settle their thoughts, but if he's making no attempt to grow or evolve, then perhaps it is time for both parties involved to part ways.

7. You feel anchored instead of his partner

If your relationship has become an everyday battleground between grounding him or fixing his issues, and you as their source, that is no relationship at all; that is full-time work for both of you.

How Can You Let Go

1. Be Honest About Your Needs

Sit him down and have an honest discussion about what you want and how his lifestyle doesn't align with your goals. Use "I" statements instead of accusatory ones when discussing this matter. Once you decide to move forward, set firm boundaries by being clear about your expectations. Don't become someone's fallback choice or emotional safety net; set clear standards.

2. Stand Firm against Charm

Mr. Mobile Home may be adept at distracting you with laughter and fun--even promising change!

3. Stay strong against their charm while staying focused on what's best for yourself and why you are parting ways with them.

4. Surround Yourself with Support

Seeking help from friends, family, or therapists to manage the breakup and realize why a relationship that respects your values would be ideal is necessary to find relief from pain.

5. Find Your Own Stability

Letting him go allows you to focus on creating the life you want, whether that's prioritizing career goals, friendships, or self-care - now is your time to thrive!

Final Thought on Mr. Mobile Home

Dating Mr. Mobile Home can be like embarking on an amusement park ride: thrilling and full of surprises yet fleeting in its duration; eventually leaving you feeling dizzy from all its moving parts.

If you prefer adventure and are open to a relationship that involves lots of travel, this might be your dream partner. But if stability and commitment are important to you, don't get involved with this wanderer; trust me, sis, that there's someone out there just as driven as yourself who deserves your affection.

Mr. Mobile Home may provide entertainment at first, but his constant movement can become unnerving over time. You aren't meant to be his anchor or life coach--you are simply partners in life.

Letting go doesn't mean you no longer care; it means prioritizing yourself over Mr. Mobile Home's needs. Once you find someone compatible, you will know you have made the correct decision in releasing him from your life. Sister, I Hope Your Ride Ended Safely. Whew, girl! Let's be honest--Mobile Homes aren't exactly safe shelters when the storms of life arise; one gust of wind or unexpected curveball from life could send everything tumbling over like soda cans in a hurricane.

Sometimes you just must put your love life on solid ground, sis. So, if you have said goodbye to Mr. Mobile Home, give yourself a pat on the back and revel in knowing you are no longer riding along on his unpredictable journey.

CHAPTER 11

Ladies, Let's Honor Our Grandmas: They Were Pioneers of Long Distance Love

To start things off right, let us recognize and thank our grandmothers. They were dating when there was no FaceTime, Zoom, or video calls--just handwritten letters with lots of trust shown between partners. Unlike me, who suffers from trust issues (yes, I see a therapist!), my grandmas would never find someone so far away that they could not trust enough for long- distance romance.

Let me paint you the picture: when he comes into town, those moments with him can be truly exciting; but then he leaves, leaving you alone with nothing but your thoughts and unanswered texts. This arrangement is ideal for the strong, independent woman who values her space; with no one to share it with and an extra-long bed to yourself, this space is your own. Ladies, meet Mr. Houseboat--he's never quite settled into an anchorage!

Dating a Houseboat Is Like Dating an Uncertain Rollercoaster!

No Stability

Like real houseboats, Mr. Houseboat seems like he's always moving. One day, you may see him; then the next thing you know, he's gone again, leaving you questioning whether to even change the sheets anymore.

Depreciation Over Time

Houseboats depreciate over time, as does your relationship. As time progresses, you realize there's no equity--just an enjoyable ride with no lasting returns.

Financing Difficulties

Emotional financing for this individual is like trying to get financing for an actual houseboat: complex, high-risk, and fraught with strings attached.

Weather Dependent

Just as storms can rock a houseboat, life's challenges will send this man drifting further away instead of anchoring down with you.

Sea Sickness

If you suffer from emotional motion sickness, this relationship could leave you feeling unsettled, queasy, and desperate to find safety in an anchorage point.

Who Should Consider Houseboat Living?

The Free Spirit: If you thrive on independence and don't mind spending long stretches alone, Mr. Houseboat might be perfect.

The Low-Maintenance Woman: For women who like living in the moment without worrying too much about long-term plans or commitments, Mr. Houseboat could be perfect.

Are You Wanting a Houseboat Partner Who Keeps Sailing Away Without Being At The Dock?

Have you decided Mr. Houseboat's endless drifting isn't for you? Sadly, life is too short to wait around for someone who keeps moving around all the time; here's how you can let him sail away while anchoring yourself into something secure and fulfilling:

Drop Your Anchor on Your Terms

Be firm about what you want from him and stick to it. If he can no longer provide stability for you, it may be best to cut his rope and let him drift. Be clear with yourself about any non-negotiables.

Have a Farewell Conversation

You don't have to make him an outcast; simply be honest in explaining that this arrangement no longer suits your needs and that a change may be needed.

*What to Say: "I care about you, but am searching for something more stable in my life. I can't keep waiting for us to connect when what I need is stability."

Block the Dock

To ensure a successful transition, do not leave room for him to return and park his houseboat on your dock. That means no "just checking in" texts, late-night calls, or "let's meet when you're back" vibes from him.

Focus on Your Stability

Now that the emotional rollercoaster has subsided, it is time to put yourself first. Establish a firm foundation, prioritize goals, and surround yourself with people who can offer consistent support and reliability.

Close the Door When Mr. Houseboat Returns

As they always do! - Be firm about shutting him out again. Suggested Statement of Departure for Response (DSR) is: "I'm glad you're doing well, but I'm looking for something different now; I have moved on."

Find Your Forever Dock

Give yourself the best chance of meeting the person who will offer love, security, and stability: your forever dock! By opening up to relationships that provide these qualities for each other. Eventually, you may discover one.

Final Thought on Mr. Houseboat

Mr. Houseboat will always remain floating from place to place, never staying long enough to build anything of lasting significance. That is his journey - let him continue sailing away while you build yourself an enjoyable, fulfilling life full of stability, love, and purpose.

Sis, you aren't here just to be someone's backup dock; instead, you are the marina itself--and the right ship will know when and how to drop its anchor and stay. Dating Mr. Houseboat may feel exciting and romantic at times when he is around, but prolonged periods of drifting, cold beds, and emotional rollercoaster rides may be too much of an emotional rollercoaster ride for many women.

If you're seeking stability, someone to stand by you through all the storms and sunshine, this might not be your match. But if you're ready for an adventurous short-term experience without strings attached - grab your life jacket and jump aboard. Just remember, sister - when things become turbulent on the seas, you deserve someone who stays put. not one who keeps drifting away!

Sis, Are You Sitting by the Dock or Taking Control?

Now it is up to you whether you want to sit idly by as the tide comes in and goes out while all your friends drink up. But let me add this: if you choose Mr. Houseboat as your partner, make sure that you still have access to FaceTime calls and any surprises from time to time!

Yes, I said pop-up! Don't take offense; as I told you previously, I have trust issues which I am working to overcome with therapy sessions, but sometimes you need to ensure the only other passenger in that boat is the GPS and not Becky or Keisha from his "gym crew."

So, if you plan to stay, keep the lines of communication open-- and perhaps keep running shoes ready just in case there are unexpected check-ins. Don't take my word for it; go check for yourself.

Let's Recap, Sis--We Have Been Through It!

Let's take a step back to remember this crazy ride we have been through together! I will say no shame is found in my game; I believe I have met every property mentioned above in my past (please don't judge me; it built my character!) Here is who we have met so far:

1. **Mr. Timeshare** - Part-time love mixed with full-time confusion.

2. **Mr. Money Pit** - An irresistibly seductive drain on your wallet and sanity.

3. **Mr. Rental Property** - Enjoy its benefits without the commitment necessary until more is wanted by you (unless that person wants more).

4. **Mr. Fixer Upper** - Has promise but, only if he's prepared to put in the work needed from him

5. **Mr. Foreclosure** - Ruined but redeemable...maybe.

6. **Mr. Bank-Owned Property** - Mom holds on tight, and you won't get anywhere with her!

7. **Mr. Houseboat** - Always drifting, never docking, leaving you seasick and single.

8. **Mr. Short Sale** - Hurriedly closing it quickly, even if not ready yet

9. **Mr. Mobile Home** - As it travels from place to place with no real destination in mind, Mr. Mobile Home keeps people guessing!

So let me tell you this: if you've made it this far and remain standing, you deserve love and happiness. Let's raise a glass to all we've learned together as well as celebrate what laughs were shared, and look forward to our brighter futures together - because our Dream Homes await!

Oh, wait, sis, before we move onto Dream Home territory, there's one last person we should discuss. This one's for my ladies who say: 'I'd rather have some piece of a man than none at all."

CHAPTER 12

Ladies, let me introduce Mr. Efficiency Apartment.

While he doesn't offer much in return for your "love," he may do as a temporary shelter when needed. While not technically homeless or dream home material, he is definitely no one-night stand material!

Dating Mr. Efficiency Apartment: The Bare Minimum Bachelor

Let's discuss Mr. Efficiency Apartment--the bachelor who gives just enough for things to remain functional but doesn't feel like home. He's like the smaller, scrappier cousin of Studio Apartment. Sure, everything necessary may technically be there, but don't expect an elaborate kitchen; at best, you might get access to one hot plate and a mini fridge!

The Vibe: His charm will draw your eye with minimal effort needed on your part. Romantic gestures might include ordering pizza for delivery and watching Netflix instead of cooking up something elaborate in front of candlelight.

Reality Check: While studio apartments may seem appealing at first, Mr. Efficiency tends to prioritize comfort over substance. If you're searching for more substances than meet the eye. However, you might feel confined.

Why Efficiency Apartment Dating Is Difficult

Compact and Convenient! At first glance, compact and convenient relationships seem ideal: minimal effort needed, quick connection time, no extraneous frills - yet this doesn't necessarily translate to lasting love or lasting relationships. Sometimes being "efficient" only means temporary happiness.

There's No Room to Grow

In relationships without enough "square footage," emotional depth, future plans, and strong foundations may be lacking. Like an efficiency apartment where everything is close by, this type of relationship lacks boundaries and may make it hard to differentiate between casual friendship and commitment. But who are these arrangements meant for?

For someone seeking something light and casual, efficiency apartment dating could be just the right way. For someone not ready to commit fully but still seeking companionship, short-term love relationships may be perfect.

Why You Deserve a Studio Apartment (or Bigger)

Although efficiency apartments serve a purpose, studio apartments provide more. Space, functionality, and possibly even full kitchen facilities allow couples to grow together more comfortably in long-term happiness relationships. While convenience can be great, comfort requires space to spread out and expand.

Final Thoughts in Mr. Efficiency Apartment.

Dear sis, stop fitting yourself into Mr. Efficiency Apartment's limited square footage - although he may

occasionally provide shelter, more love, effort, and room for growth are in order. Leave Mr. Efficiency Apartment behind and start building that relationship mansion you have been dreaming of!

Just remember, you don't want to settle for just a microwave and a Murphy bed; what you really desire is a full kitchen, backyard, and someone ready to share all aspects of their house as well as their heart with you.

CHAPTER 13

Are You Prepared for Your Dream Home?

Now that we have successfully navigated the dating real estate market and we are finally prepared to buy our Dream Homes, let's talk about preparation. Don't ask for luxury mansions while offering nothing other than smiles and prayers as contributions; even when buying real homes, you must come prepared!

Step 1: Assess Your Credit (aka Emotional Baggage)

It's just as if it would be foolish to buy a house with credit scores of 500, so why embark on relationships, dragging drama from past relationships? If there are still trust issues, unresolved heartbreak, or you tend to ghost people often then now is the time for self-awareness work to be done; love is the prize, but self-knowledge should always come first.

Step 2: Save for Your Down Payment (Invest in Yourself)

Finding your Dream Home (or Dream Man) won't happen magically. To make sure it does happen for you, put forth effort into being attractive as a catch yourself, by setting goals, being happy, and building emotional stability - two solid people build a dream relationship together, not one incomplete structure on top of another one.

Step 3: Be Realistic About Your Wish List

Sure, you want your perfect partner to be tall, rich, funny, emotionally intelligent, and capable of cooking like Gordon Ramsay--but let's face it: even dream homes have some imperfections. What really matters is understanding which qualities (such as stability, respect, or loyalty) you need as opposed to which are mere extras (six-pack abs or private jet).

Step 4: Discover What You Contribute

It is impossible to expect to meet a true soul mate if your own energy doesn't match that dream partner you desire, so ask yourself these questions:

*Are You Kind and Supportive of Others?

*Are Your Goals Aligned with Theirs?

If the answer to these questions is "no," it may be time to level up: make sure the table you sit at matches up with what he expects of You!

Step 5: Prepare For The Work Ahead

Even dream homes require ongoing upkeep. Don't expect it to clean itself! Likewise, relationships require constant communication, compromise, and effort to stay alive!

Let's be Real: Let me set you straight: there is no such thing as perfection in life or love--nor in that man you've been envisioning on Pinterest boards. And guess what: neither you nor I am perfect either--and that's okay; love is not about finding someone flawless; rather, it should be about finding someone whose quirks, imperfections, and personality make your heart feel at home.

Why Perfection Isn't the Goal

No One Is Perfect (And That Is Beautiful). Are you really expecting your partner to expect you to always be perfect, without unmanageable hair days, funky moods, or nights when ordering pizza is preferable to cooking? Of course, not - so why hold him to an impossible standard you wouldn't expect for yourself?

Perfection Is Fatiguing

Attaining perfection can be exhausting, like trying to keep white carpets in a house with children and animals. Real relationships thrive through authenticity rather than unattainable ideals.

Flaws Create Connection

Sometimes it is the little imperfections-his goofy laugh, your love of off-key singing or his knack of burning toast every time-that make our relationships real and unique.

How to Let Go of the "Perfect" Fantasy

Focus on Core Values

Look for someone who shares your core values - respect, kindness, and communication- rather than superficial must-haves such as six-figure incomes or perfect abs. Use the 80/20 Rule. No one is perfect, and that's okay; nobody gets 100% right the first time around.

Be Honest About Your Flaws

Acknowledging your imperfections and their impact on relationships. Recognize and acknowledge your imperfections as they may impact the relationships growth. Finding your ideal partner doesn't require finding someone "perfect," it means finding one who understands and embraces all your quirks, complements your strengths, and loves you through any weaknesses.

Sis, let me be the one to tell you this truth--there's no such thing as perfect. No one's perfect--including you--which is okay. Love isn't about finding someone flawless; rather, it should be about finding someone whose quirks, imperfections, and personality fit your heart just perfectly. Your dream doesn't involve finding an ideal partner; instead, it should involve two flawed individuals working towards creating something beautiful together, one step at a time. So let go of your idea of perfection and embrace the reality of real relationships while remembering: the greatest love stories are written within their imperfections.

Your goal should not be perfection but instead an everlasting love that lasts a lifetime - that is where the real magic lies!

Sis, It Is Time to Assess Yourself and Build That Dream Home!

Now that we've conducted the necessary soul searching, set our boundaries, and survived a seemingly never-ending stream of "Mr. Not-Quite-It," it is time to focus on the prize: our dream home. Here is where everything makes sense - heartbreaks and lessons learned are no longer remembered fondly- now that your true prince has arrived!

What Does It Mean When Discussing Love?

Your Dream Home-in-love doesn't just refer to aesthetics - it's about how it makes you feel! Your ideal partner makes you feel safe, valued, and at peace, no matter the state of things in the world today. Your ideal space provides comfort, laughter, and love. It is everything you have been hoping for since the dark days you thought would never arrive!

Building Your Dream Home Step by Step

A strong relationship, like a sturdy house, requires a firm foundation. That means building upon trust, respect, communication, and shared values as the cornerstones. Without these, walls may collapse with even minor storms. For the best building process: prioritize functionality over flash.

Sure, tall, dark, and handsome might be on your wish list, but what about kind, loyal, emotionally available people as well? Your Dream Home shouldn't just be about flash - it should provide support and nourish your life in every aspect. Your Dream Home doesn't need to look exactly like anyone else's - it should reflect who you are as an individual, rather than follow what is currently popular or Instagrammable.

Ongoing Maintenance

Even Dream Homes need constant upkeep. Relationships need effort, compromise and love in order to remain strong and grow stronger over time. By keeping what you've built for the long haul, its beauty will endure for generations.

Once You Find Your Dream Home

Once you discover your ideal partner, everything makes sense. No longer do you question the journey, heartaches, and detours along the way--they all lead up to this person--one who makes you feel as if home has finally been found.

Relationships don't need to be about perfection; they should bring peace. Finding someone who sees your worth and enriches your life beyond imagination should be your aim.

Your Dream Home (so You Don't Lose It)

Finding your ideal home is only the first step - now comes the hard part of keeping it standing strong! Just like with relationships, Dream Homes require regular care, maintenance, and effort in order to remain standing strong - otherwise cracks will appear and before long, you may face foreclosure of both mind and heart! Let's work together so this doesn't happen!

1. Regularly Recheck Trust and Communication

Why It Matters: To keep the health of any relationship, its foundation (trust, respect, and communication) needs regular evaluation to still be strong.

How to Do It: Engage in honest dialogues, address concerns early, and don't allow small cracks to turn into major ones.

2. Make Early Repairs, Not Ignore Issues

Why It Matters: Putting off repairs won't solve a leaky faucet; rather, it will flood the house. Unresolved relationship issues have the same outcome.

How to Do It: Approach conflicts head-on, work to find solutions together, and, if needed, bring in a professional (such as a therapist) to help mend what has broken.

3. Keep It Clean (Respect and Appreciation)

Why It Matters: Clutter can transform even the coziest home into chaos, just as emotional clutter--resentments, unspoken tensions, or taking each other for granted--can do the same in relationships.

How to Do It: Express gratitude towards your partner,

acknowledge their efforts, and address small annoyances as soon as they occur.

4. Upgrade As Needed (Growth and Change)

Why It Matters: Just as our homes change over time, so too should relationships. Stagnation can lead to dissatisfaction, which ultimately devalues both relationships.

How to Do It: Encourage each other's personal development, accept change, and find ways to keep the spark alive - whether through trying new activities together or setting new goals as a couple - keep building your future together.

5. Keep Utilities Running (With Love and Effort)

Why It Matters: Neglecting basic needs like kindness, love, and effort could leave your dream home feeling cold and dark.

How To Do It: Regularly express love, set aside quality time together, and put forth effort to keep the relationship strong.

6. Protect Your Investment (Commitments and Boundaries)

Why It Matters: Just like you protect your home with insurance, protecting relationships requires commitment and boundaries.

How To Do It: Show loyalty and respect for each other as individuals while setting clear boundaries to keep outside forces from disrupting their foundation.

7. Weather the Storms Together (Resilience)

Why it Matters: Every relationship faces challenges--financial stresses, family drama, or just the ups and downs of everyday life can all make life harder on any couple. How you deal with these storms will decide whether your dream home stays together or disintegrates into its parts.

CHAPTER 14

For The Men Still on The Market

Gentlemen, it's time for us to talk. While this book was intended mainly for my female readers, some of you do show these "property" traits. This book was intended to help female readers first and foremost, but that does not mean I won't offer advice for you, too! Don't worry--I have plenty of advice in store!

Now, let me be clear. If you find this book on your friend's nightstand or she suddenly starts yelling "You are such a Timeshare!" now you know the source of their frustration. But let's switch roles; maybe you recognize yourself in this role and are having second thoughts about being one, or you want to stay one but aren't sure how best to discuss this with those closest to you. This book could give the answers.

Or perhaps--and this is significant--you have decided that upgrading is in your plans; that your home can become someone's dream home. After all, being on the market too long can cause its value to decrease--something no one wants! Even if you're a Foreclosure or Fixer-Upper, you still have value. To unlock it, the key lies in understanding your ideal property type and making changes necessary for greater worth - whether that means becoming your Dream Home or taking on timeshare roles with pride; remembering that value begins within yourself!

At first, let me emphasize this point for all men: always be honest when dating women. Nobody has time, energy, or patience for detective work--nobody wants to wear a lie detector belt around their hip or install GPS trackers in their car only to discover they've been lying about something or found out that one or both parties are deceitful.

That can be tiresome; we aren't dealing with Netflix crime thrillers here--this is real life and emotions being played out here. So, save everyone the drama by being honest: If you aren't ready to settle down yet, say that; if your lifestyle includes Timeshare living versus "Dream Home," own that as well; if there is still baggage unresolved on either side that needs addressing immediately (i.e, leaking roof), let her know!

Honesty may not make you look good, but it will always make you respectable--and that will last longer than a smooth line and great haircut. So cut the games and be truthful; no one has time for "Where were you last night?" interrogations or strange receipts turning up in unexpected places. Being honest is more than just the best policy; it's essential for protecting property value, so swindling away with lies could cost your home dearly in foreclosure proceedings. Stay honest, open, and save the mystery for the escape rooms-not relationships!

Before anyone begins shouting that they've told a woman they weren't interested in settling down, yet she still wants to invest in this property! --let me just clarify one thing. Yes, ladies--if you disregarded the open house disclaimer that said the property wasn't for sale that weekend--that is on you; but for now, let me focus on communicating my message directly to men.

Listen closely: if she insists on something you do not wish

for--such as a committed relationship, future together, or simply brunch every weekend--then you must intervene to stop it. Change locks, place up a **NO TRESPASSING** sign, and end all ties at once.

Why? Otherwise you risk setting yourself up for potential disaster-not only awkward text message scenarios but even potentially fatal attraction scenarios (nobody wants a boiled bunny on their stove! Google it and get the reference, trust me). Doing the right thing doesn't require being cold or mean; it just requires being clear. If you aren't into something, take steps to protect both your peace and hers by leaving no "what ifs." Otherwise, you might end up on Dateline explaining how it "never came." Save yourself the drama: lock that metaphorical or literal door behind her and toss away its key if she does not understand. Keeping things 100 is beneficial for both parties involved!

Let's be real: if you're broke, admit it. There's no shame in admitting your situation in life; instead, let's call it what it is: instead of needing someone romantically, perhaps what you need most right now is someone to help pay your rent and share the costs with. Don't fall for romance; search for payday loan companies instead of romantic relationships! I think my point has been made.

Love is wonderful, but it won't pay the electric bill. Candlelit dinners may look romantic, but if they're your only source of illumination because you didn't pay your electric bill on time, it becomes problematic. Don't talk about "building a future together" when your credit score is barely holding together, and your savings account has become practically nonexistent.

Prioritize getting your financial house in order before trying to move someone in. Love cannot be built upon debts and bounced checks--that would be like trying to build on quicksand! Instead, take some time away and hustle hard, save and stabilize; once you can offer more than half of the Netflix bills again, then come back around the table; until then, it may just be financial help that you look for instead of true love. Prioritize accordingly!

Let's talk about self-worth: you should appreciate yourself as well. Stop treating yourselves like some sort of 24-hour roadside motel that welcomes anyone and everyone - you are not a hotel!

Think about it: hotels get used, abused, and left with an upheaval when the guests leave. Is that how you want to live? With no standards or exclusiveness for anyone passing through who might offer an interesting story or smile? Nah, king--you deserve better. Your Dream Home with gated access and premium amenities deserves more consideration than that from everyone who enters. Not everyone deserves access.

Renting yourself out to everyone erodes your value; people come to you only for quick fixes, not long-term investments; that doesn't lead to love, respect, or enjoyment--that's wear and tear. You deserve someone who sees your worth and treats you accordingly, rather than treating you like an Airbnb until they find something "better."

Setting high standards, increasing property values, and remembering to never let anyone crash for the night will ensure you build an empire instead of renting yourself out as an uninvited guest. Value yourself first so others will respect you; otherwise, there will always be space available for something ridiculous like "vacancy for nonsense." No vacancy! Period.

CHAPTER 15

Can Friends and Family Help with the Home-buying Process—or Are They Just Adding Drama?

Imagine this: you're finally ready to enter the wild world of home-buying. You've watched the home-buying shows and seen beautiful hardwood floors, open concept kitchens, and dreamy bay windows where you'll sip coffee every morning - but now comes the tough question: should someone go with me as I begin this adventure? Perhaps a trusted friend, your mother, or even one of your cousins who likes pointing out flaws would be beneficial in providing impartial opinions!

Now this could go either way; it could be beneficial or catastrophic. On one hand, having someone accompany you could serve as your own personal inspector - they could point out things you might otherwise miss, like "Hey, did you notice that crack in the foundation?" and "How much would it cost to replace that roof?" (Translation: You sure you want this Fixer Upper?), but sometimes we need that voice of reason recommending against purchasing houses that could easily become condemned with just one gust of wind!

Bringing along the wrong person can turn your homebuying dream into an epic drama. We all know that friend who acts like they're an interior designer and tours every home, saying things like, "Oh, I would knock this wall down," or "This home would look better with Spanish tile decor." But ma'am--this decision doesn't revolve around you--you aren't signing your mortgage agreement!

Family can also be an issue. While inviting your mom can seem like a great idea at first glance, she may start making passive-aggressive comments such as, "Well if it were me, I'd find something closer," or asking whether "Are you sure this is what you want? It's a big responsibility," which might leave you questioning your life plan altogether or at the very least whether to remain living in your current space indefinitely.

At the core of it all lies one key truth: you are ultimately responsible for any decisions about bringing someone along or not. When plumbing goes haywire or neighbors party past 3 a.m. on Tuesdays, it falls squarely on you to address those problems-- not them. While extra eyes may help to keep an eye out, ultimately this decision belongs to you alone and should remain your decision alone.

Conclusion -Bringing someone along can be extremely useful, but be wary about who you invite - choose someone who knows and respects both you and your vision while not trying to take over everything themselves. A co-pilot rather than someone shouting questions such as, "Are you sure this neighborhood suits your tastes?" is key in your pursuit.

And if you decide to do it on your own, that is okay too - sometimes staying independent from outside influences is the smart move. After all, it is YOU who pays the bills, deals with any sort of behavior in the house and creates a home! So, when making your choice or, considering real estate of love as a choice, choose carefully or at the very least, prepare yourself for a bit of drama. Home buying for love has taught us one thing - everyone has an opinion, even if their name isn't on the deed!

Taking Advice from Family: No One Tells the Truth Like Your Kids

If you think your friends or parents can be blunt in their honesty, let me introduce the ultimate truth-tellers: your kids. No sugarcoating, no diplomacy--they speak the truth without filter or diplomatic pretense--when it comes to real estate decisions, they will certainly voice their opinions!

Imagine showing your kids the house you're considering with great anticipation; everything seems fantastic: granite countertops and an ample backyard; then your eight-year-old walks into their bedroom and declares: "This is it? I've seen closets bigger than this!" or worse still - "This place is creepy!" Children rarely hold back when speaking their minds - they'll tell you exactly how they feel without trying to soften the blow!

But kids don't just make things difficult on purpose: their ability to notice things adults may overlook allows them to notice aspects you often overlook, such as space requirements and commute times that they care more about than your calculations on square footage or commute times. Kids consider details such as "Where will I ride my bike?" and "Will there be friends nearby?" Ultimately, comfort matters--if your little one isn't happy, neither are you!

As such, it's crucial that your real estate of love decision takes them into consideration. Finding a house isn't just about finding one you like - but finding somewhere they thrive too! So, before making your choice, ask yourself this important question:

Are we creating an environment in which they'll come to love or are we forcing it on them? Will they feel at ease here, or will there be years of complaining that "our old house or relationship was better?"

Now, this doesn't mean letting go of control completely to your children; that would likely result in you living next to Disneyland or in an entire candy house! But their point of view should still be considered; perhaps their soccer dreams require larger space; or maybe that cozy bedroom you find attractive simply doesn't allow enough room for their beloved dinosaur collection.

On the flipside, don't let their first resistance discourage you too quickly. Change can be hard on children, even for the best house in the world; initially, they may resist moving into your new place and liking your new bae; it is important to figure out whether this resistance is just a temporary adjustment phase or something more permanent.

Just keep this in mind - children can surprise us! A seemingly creepy neighborhood could quickly become their favorite once they discover the park or make friends on nearby streets. At the end of the day, you are the decision-maker, but it is wise to involve your kids. While you think about property taxes and school districts, they're thinking about their daily lives in your new house - and their happiness will help to create an enjoyable atmosphere.

Before signing any papers and making that relationship official, take some time to listen to what your little truth-tellers have to say. Their opinions might surprise or amuse you--at the very least, they will give you something amusing when later they tell you they should've listened!

CHAPTER 16

Closing Day

Let's be clear: this journey through the real estate of love was not meant to judge or bash, but to bring clarity, humor, and wisdom. Like buying or selling property, relationships can be stressful, yet exhilarating experiences filled with unexpected twists and surprises; ultimately, though, it all comes down to knowing what you want and offering as well as accepting from a partner.

Let's go back over our list of properties and consider what lessons they have taught us:

1. **Mr. Timeshare**
   Lesson: Great for short-term fun, but don't expect full-time commitment.

2. **Mr. Rental Property**
   Lesson: If marriage is your goal, make sure this arrangement aligns with your plans.

3. **Mr. Rent-to-Own**
   Lesson: He talks long-term but lives month-to-month. Don't mistake potential for a plan—make sure the lease comes with a real commitment.

4. **Mr. Money Pit**
   Lesson: If love costs you your peace (and all your coins), it's time to move on.

5. **Mr. Fixer-Upper**
   Lesson: Only invest if he's willing to put in the work, too—

otherwise, it's not worth your time.

6. **Mr. Foreclosure**
Lesson: You can't fix someone who won't take the first step for themselves.

7. **Mr. Short Sale**
Lesson: Proceed with caution—love is a journey, not a race.

8. **Mr. Bank-Owned Property**
Lesson: Unless he's ready to cut the cord, you'll always feel like the third wheel.

9. **Mr. Mobile Home**
Lesson: Flexibility is great, but stability is better.

10. **Mr. Houseboat**
Lesson: Fun for the ride, but don't expect him to dock anytime soon.

11. **Mr. Efficiency Apartment**
Lesson: Don't settle for scraps when you deserve the whole feast.

The Final Walkthrough

Closing chapters in relationships is also stressful. Paperwork must be reviewed, fine print reviewed, and whispers of unease may arise--yet ignoring such warning signs will only lead to buyer's regret in either real estate or love transactions.

Ladies, some of you may need to tour all these properties on this list before finding your Dream Home. Though this process can be exhausting, each experience teaches something about what you want versus don't want and which properties won't do the trick for you. Don't give up; each property reveals something valuable about who you are as an individual and how far you will go to find what you want.

Fellas, you might find yourself holding several properties before being ready to become someone's Dream Home. That's okay--growth takes time. Just don't forget the work involved--no one wants their property to sit unsold forever on the market!

Advice for the Road

Before entering any relationship, ask yourself:

- Does this align with what I genuinely want?
- Am I ignoring red flags because the view is nice?
- Do I feel at peace, or am I constantly negotiating my standards?

Reality Check: Some people should only stay in your life for 30 days and not 30 years. Like touring a house and quickly realizing "This isn't it," but learning something useful from it all, nonetheless.

Look out for signs--whether it be "for sale," "no trespassing," or "Dream Home" signs--and trust your gut when making decisions about buying or renting property. Real Estate of Love doesn't involve searching for the ideal home; rather, it involves finding what works for you. So go out there, explore the market, and find your forever home!

One key point to keep in mind: your pen is in your hands; don't feel pressured into signing on if a deal doesn't feel right for you. Sure, the agent (or person you're dating) may seem nice enough and say all the right things, but if your gut tells you otherwise - listen to your instinct. Contracts may bind, but regret is something we all must live with for life.

Love, like real estate, comes with its share of pressure. People will tell you it's an awesome opportunity! Or "You may never find something better!" but desperation is never good in relationships or real estate transactions - don't rush into anything just because someone talks quickly or the property looks appealing; keep this in mind: even the prettiest properties may contain termites!

It's OK to walk away. It's okay to say, "I need more time to think." And it is entirely acceptable to demand an inspection (metaphorically, of course) before making your commitment. Finding the ideal property or person won't leave you feeling rushed, pressured, or settling for less than you deserve.

Let's be honest--everyone makes mistakes; sometimes the wrong one appears more tempting than the others, and you might ask yourself whether saying no was worth the sacrifice. Every time you choose yourself and your long-term happiness over short-term convenience is a win!

Now let's end this with some humor; real estate can be unpredictable and confusing when searching for love, often leading to absurd circumstances and unexpected turns of events. As you attempt to locate your Dream Home while dodging Mobile Homes, Money Pits, Short Sales, etc, it can be exhausting but ultimately hilarious when looking back - one day you will recall all those times Mr. Efficiency Apartment almost signed the contract but couldn't commit to a proper date and you will laugh about them all!

Here's the bottom line: life and love are full of choices; only you can decide when, where, and with whom you commit. Don't let anyone pressure you into signing on the dotted line if something feels wrong: when the right partner arrives - who might just become your Dream Home - signing won't feel like pressure but instead like peace.

People, the real estate of love is always available. Best wishes as you explore your options; don't forget that finding your Dream Home may take longer than expected! As you search, try not to forget to have some fun a and laugh along the way!

CHAPTER 17

Quotes for My Ladies

On Timeshares:

- "Papa was a rolling stone. Honey, Papa was a Timeshare—here today, gone tomorrow."
- "A Timeshare might offer you a little fun in the sun, but when the season's over, so is he."

On Money Pits:

- "Love shouldn't come with hidden fees and surprise repairs—ditch the Money Pit before you're bankrupt in more ways than one."
- "You're not his ATM, and if you are, it's time to put a lock on the account."

On Fixer-Uppers:

- "He's got potential, sure—but so does a sinking ship if you've got enough duct tape."
- "If he needs a full renovation, make sure he's not handing you the toolbox while he watches Netflix."

On Efficiency Apartments:

- "If he's only giving you the bare minimum, it's time to upgrade to luxury living."

- "Girl, stop accepting breadcrumbs when you deserve the whole bakery."

On Houseboats:
- "He's adventurous, exciting, and always moving—just don't let him capsize your plans."
- "A Houseboat will take you places, but don't forget to ask: where are we docking?"

On Short Sales:
- "He's rushing to close the deal but remember love is not about who signs first—it's about who stays."
- "A discount might sound tempting, but can you afford the emotional repairs?"

On Mobile Homes:
- "If he's always on the move, don't let your heart get a ride without knowing the destination."
- "Love shouldn't feel like a road trip with no GPS—don't get lost chasing a Mobile Home."

On Dream Homes:
- "He's the one you've been searching for—so stop looking out the window waiting for a better offer."
- "Dream Homes exist, but don't turn it into a nightmare by doubting the blessing."

www.ingramcontent.com/pod-product-compliance
Lightning Source LLC
Chambersburg PA
CBHW050649160426
43194CB00010B/1873